CLASSIC ELITE
Shawls, Wraps & Scarves
20 IDEAS • 3 WAYS

sixth&springbooks New York

To Chelsea

● Who brought laughter into our workplace, adored the creative process, and sometimes ate cake for breakfast.

sixth&springbooks

161 Avenue of the Americas, New York, NY 10013

Editorial Director
JOY AQUILINO

Photography
JACK DEUTSCH

Senior Editor
MICHELLE BREDESON

Technical Illustrations
ULI MONCH

Art Director
DIANE LAMPHRON

Stylist
KHALIAH JONES

Yarn Editor
CHRISTINA BEHNKE

Hair & Makeup
Sokphalla Ban

Instructions Editors
LISA BUCCELLATO
JEANNIE CHIN
BARBARA KHOURI
AMY POLCYN
LORI STEINBERG

Vice President, Publisher
TRISHA MALCOLM

Creative Director
JOE VIOR

Instructions Proofreaders
STEPHANIE MRSE
CHARLOTTE PARRY
JUDITH SLOAN

Production Manager
DAVID JOINNIDES

President
ART JOINNIDES

Copy Editor
LISA SILVERMAN

ISBN: 978-1-936096-52-7

Library of Congress Control Number: 2012947640

Manufactured in China

1 3 5 7 9 10 8 6 4 2

First Edition

Classic Elite Yarns

www.classiceliteyarns.com

Contents

Easy Stripes
page 10
1 Striped shawl 12
2 Striped shawlette 15
3 Striped cowl 15

Jewel Tones
page 16
1 Buttoned neck wrap 18
2 Shawlette 19
3 Coat scarf 20

Pretty in Pink
page 22
1 Swirl-edged stole 24
2 Single-repeat scarf 26
3 Multiple-repeat scarf 27

Block Party
page 28
1 Asymmetrical shrug 30
2 Block & garter scarf 32
3 Cowlneck capelet 35

The Magic of Transformation

How many times have you heard beginner knitters say, "I can't really knit, I can only make scarves"? "Only scarves"? How did an accessory so versatile, so stylish, and so adaptable fall by the wayside? The scarf should be celebrated, not dismissed as a glorified rectangle. Change the shape and it's a shawl. Increase the surface area and it becomes a wrap. Sew the ends together or add some shaping and it can be a cowl, a capelet, or even a poncho. Yes, the lowly scarf is capable of complete transformation.

Transformation is the theme of this book. Isn't knitting itself a transformation? It's only natural to draw a comparison between knitting and alchemy, the magical process of turning something ordinary into gold. Every handknitted piece is made using the most rudimentary tools: sticks and some string. Every texture is created with, essentially, a combination of knit and purl stitches. The magic occurs when you let your imagination take over.

The designers featured here were tasked with taking a single idea and transforming it into three different looks. These projects started with a tiny spark of inspiration . . . a silhouette, a stitch pattern, a technique. Then, each designer's "collection" became an exploration of that theme. A look through the designs reveals swatches conceived and reconceived in wild textures and colors and in a variety of shapes. You'll find multidirectional knits and fabric sculpted into three dimensions, surprising constructions, and unexpected design elements. Eyelets and lace emerge from chunky wool and ethereal mohair alike.

The sixty designs range from cute to whimsical to elegant. Of course, you'll find the usual suspects, such as *Silky Alpaca Lace* and *MountainTop Vail*, knit into the lace patterns they lend themselves to so well. But what about a striped cowl in chunky, organic cotton *Sprout*? Or a lace pattern knit in light-as-air mohair *Pirouette* alongside the same pattern in bulky, single-ply extrafine merino *Ariosa*? It's all about transformation.

The wide variety of projects in this book begs the question: Why do scarves seem so simple to beginners? Could it be their size? One of the best things about scarves, shawls, and wraps is that no yarn is too funky and no technique is too difficult when you're working on such a seemingly small canvas (though many a knitter will tell you that the "scarves are small" line of thinking is a total fallacy). A small project such as a cowl or a scarf presents the perfect opportunity to take a chance with a color you would never wear in a garment. Another reason to cast on is the opportunity to try a technique that has always intimidated you. Cables? Piece of cake. Lace? Sure! Colorwork? Why not? In any case, you're sure to find something that suits your taste. Take some time to flip through these pages and follow the creative journeys of the seventeen designers featured in this book. You just might be surprised.

Betsy Perry

Betsy Perry, PRESIDENT AND OWNER, CLASSIC ELITE YARNS

Three times
as nice

By each taking a single idea—a stitch, a yarn, or both, as with Linda Medina's *Block Party* — and transforming it into three fabulous designs, the designers featured here have created an inspirational collection of knitterly ingenuity. See page 28.

The Projects

•Easy Stripes

Stripe it rich with SUSAN MILLS s openwork wraps. Two shades of variegated yarn in each knit give the impression of many colors with minimal effort.

1 In soft tones of moss, indigo, and dust, this STRIPED SHAWL knit in *Alpaca Sox* makes a sumptuous addition to any outfit, any time of the year.

2 This STRIPED SHAWLETTE knit in *Liberty Wool Light* can also be worn kerchief-style by wrapping it around the neck from front to back to front and tying in the front.

3 The bright colors in this STRIPED COWL knit in variegated *Liberty Wool Light* lend a perfect contrast to the biting days of fall or winter.

SHAWL

With A, cast on 3 sts. Knit 7 rows. Rotate piece and pick up and knit 3 sts along side edge and 3 sts along cast-on edge—9 sts total.

Row 1 (RS) K3, yo, pm, k3, pm, yo, k3—11 sts.
Rows 2 and 4 Knit, slipping markers.
Row 3 K3, yo, k1, yo, slip marker, k3, slip marker, yo, k1, yo, k3—15 sts.

BEGIN PATTERN

***Row 1 (RS) K3, yo, knit to marker, yo, sm, k3, sm, yo, knit to last 3 sts, yo, k3—4 sts inc.
Rows 2 and 4 Knit, slipping markers.
Row 3 K3, yo, *k2tog, yo; rep from * to 1 st before marker, k1, yo, sm, k3, sm, yo, k1, **yo, k2tog; rep from ** to last 3 sts, yo, k3—4 sts inc.
Rows 5–8 Rep rows 1–4.
Change to B and rep rows 1–8.
Change to A.
Rep from *** until desired size or almost out of yarn. Work rows 1–2 twice in A, then twice in B. Bind off.

FINISHING

Weave in ends. Block to measurements. ●

---

❶ Striped Shawl

KNITTED MEASUREMENTS
Width approx 62"/157.5cm, or desired size
Depth approx 34"/86cm, or desired size

MATERIALS
● 1 3½oz/100g hank (each approx 450yd/411m) of Classic Elite Yarns *Alpaca Sox* (alpaca/merino/nylon) each in #1873 wedgewood brindle (A) and #1879 indigo patina (B) 🔟

● One size 4 (3.5mm) circular needle, 29"/75cm long, OR
SIZE TO OBTAIN GAUGE
● Stitch markers

GAUGE
21 sts and 42 rows to 4"/10cm over stitch pat using size 4 (3.5mm) needle, after blocking.
TAKE TIME TO CHECK GAUGE.

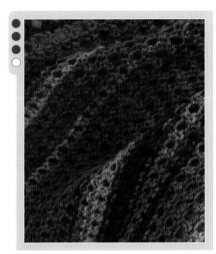

2 Striped Shawlette

KNITTED MEASUREMENTS
Width approx 34¼"/87cm
Depth approx 17"/43cm

MATERIALS
- 1 1¾oz/50g ball (each approx 200yd/183m) of Classic Elite Yarns *Liberty Wool Light* (washable wool) each in #6699 cloudy dawn (A) and #6693 rainforest (B)
- One size 4 (3.5mm) circular needle, 29"/75 cm long OR SIZE TO OBTAIN GAUGE
- Stitch markers

GAUGE
21 sts and 42 rows to 4"/10cm over stitch pat using size 4 (3.5mm) needles, after blocking.
TAKE TIME TO CHECK GAUGE.

SHAWLETTE
With A, cast on 3 sts. Knit 7 rows. Rotate piece and pick up and knit 3 sts along side edge and 3 sts along cast-on edge—9 sts total.
Row 1 (RS) K3, yo, pm, k3, pm, yo, k3—11 sts.

Rows 2 and 4 Knit, slipping markers.
Row 3 K3, yo, k1, yo, slip marker, k3, yo, slip marker, k1, yo, k1, k3—15 sts.

BEGIN PATTERN
***Row 1 (RS)** K3, yo, knit to marker, yo, sm, k3, sm, yo, knit to last 3 sts, yo, k3—4 sts inc.
Rows 2 and 4 Knit, slip markers
Row 3 K3, yo, *k2tog, yo; rep from * to 1 st before marker, k1, yo, sm, k3, sm, yo, k1, **yo, k2tog; rep from ** to last 3 sts, yo, k3—4 sts inc.
Rows 5–8 Rep rows 1–4. Change to B and rep rows 1–8. Change to A. Rep from *** six times more—239 sts. Work rows 1–2 twice in A, then twice in B—255 sts. Bind off.

FINISHING
Weave in ends. Block to measurements. ●

3 Striped Cowl

KNITTED MEASUREMENTS
Circumference approx 46"/117cm
Depth approx 12"/30.5cm

MATERIALS
- 2 1¾oz/50g balls (each approx

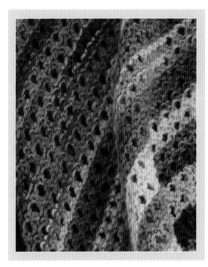

200yd/183m) of Classic Elite *Liberty Wool Light* (washable wool) each in #6698 blue twilight (A) and #6606 reflecting pool (B)
- One pair size 4 (3.5mm) needles OR SIZE TO OBTAIN GAUGE

GAUGE
21 sts and 42 rows to 4"/10cm over stitch pat using size 4 (3.5mm) needles, after blocking.
TAKE TIME TO CHECK GAUGE.

COWL
With A, cast on 63 sts.
Row 1 (RS) K3, yo, knit to last 4 sts, k2tog, k2.
Rows 2 and 4 Knit.
Row 3 (RS) K3, yo, *k2tog, yo; rep from * to last 4 sts, k2tog, k2.
Rows 5–8 Rep rows 1–4.
Change to B and rep rows 1–8.
Change to A.
Rep from ** until piece measures 46"/117cm, ending with row 8 and B. Bind off.

FINISHING
Sew cast-on edge to bind-off edge. Weave in ends. Block. ●

•Jewel Tones

NITZA COTO creates a treasure trove of gorgeous designs knit in gem-colored shades of *Magnolia*. Each of these luxurious accessories features a cable and lace pattern and feminine ruffles.

1 Stitched in a luminous shade of emerald green, this BUTTONED NECK WRAP is a simple rectangle that buttons to create a cozy neck warmer.

2 This sapphire SHAWLETTE is knit in one piece from the top down. The cable and lace panel runs down the back, adding subtle detail.

3 A buttoned amethyst COAT SCARF creates an elegant and practical layer that peeps out from under your winter coat.

STITCH GLOSSARY

kf&b Knit into front and back of st.
6-st RC Sl 3 sts to cn and hold in back, k3, k3 from cn.

PROVISIONAL CAST-ON

With waste yarn, cast on desired number of sts. Work in St st for 4 rows.

NECK WRAP

Cast on 32 sts using the provisional cast-on. Change to main yarn.
Knit 10 rows.
Row 1 (RS) K4, yo, sl 2 sts purlwise, k1, pass 2 sl sts over k st, yo, place marker (pm), work row 1 of lace chart (opposite page) over next 18 sts, pm, yo, sl 2 sts purlwise, k1, pass 2 sl sts over k st, yo, k4.
Row 2 (WS) K4, p3, slip marker (sm), work row 2 of chart, sm, p3, k4.
Cont in pats as est until 7 repeats of chart have been completed, then work rows 1–15 of chart, removing markers on last row. Knit 3 rows.
Next (buttonhole) row (RS) K9, yo, k2tog, k11, yo, k2tog, k8.
Knit 6 rows, purl 1 row.

RUFFLED EDGE

Next (inc) row (RS) K1, *kf&b; rep from * to last st, k1—62 sts.
Work 10 rows in St st. Knit 2 rows.
Bind off on WS knitwise. With RS facing, remove waste yarn from provisional cast-on and place sts on needle.
Knit 1 row, purl 1 row. Work ruffled edge as before.

FINISHING

Weave in ends. Arrange the ruffle folds and pin them to hold their shape while blocking. Block lightly. With RS facing, sew first button to right-hand garter edge 3½"/9cm up from bottom of scarf (including ruffle), then sew second button 2½"/ 6.5cm above. ●

1 Buttoned Neck Wrap

KNITTED MEASUREMENTS

Width 5½"/14cm
Length 25¼"/64cm Long

MATERIALS

- 2 1¾oz/50g balls (each approx 120yd/110m) of Classic Elite Yarns *Magnolia* (merino/silk) in #5494 deep fern (**3**)
- One pair size 6 (4mm) needles OR SIZE TO OBTAIN GAUGE
- One size 6 (4mm) circular needle, 24"/60cm long
- Cable needle (cn)
- Two ¾"/19mm buttons
- Waste yarn
- Stitch markers

GAUGE

22 sts and 32 rows = 4"/10cm
St over St st.
TAKE TIME TO CHECK GAUGE.

STITCH GLOSSARY
kf&b Knit into the front and back of st.
6-st RC Sl 3 sts to cn and hold in back, k3, k3 from cn.

SET-UP ROWS
Cast on 3 sts. Knit 36 rows, rotate needles 45 degrees to the left (do not turn), pick up 18 sts from the garter columns in knitted rows. Rotate needle again and pick up 3 sts from the cast-on edge—24 sts.
Next row (WS) K2, purl to last 2 sts, k2.

SHAWLETTE
Row 1 (inc) (RS) K2, place marker (pm), yo, k1, yo, pm, work row 1 of lace chart over next 18 sts, pm, yo, k1, yo, pm, k2—28 sts.
Row 2 (WS) K2, slip marker (sm), purl to next marker, sm, work row 2 of chart, sm, purl to next marker, sm, k2.
Row 3 (inc) (RS) K2, sm, yo, k to next marker, yo, sm, work chart as est, sm, yo, knit to next marker, yo, sm, k2—32 sts. Work as established through row 22. Rep rows 1 to 22 five times, then work rows 1–15 of chart once more—276 sts. Remove markers while working last row.

GARTER EDGE
Row 1 (WS) Knit.
Row 2 (inc) (RS) K2, kf&b, knit to last 3 sts, kf&b, k2—278 sts. Rep rows 1 and 2 four times more—286 sts.
Next row (WS) Purl.

RUFFLED EDGE
Next (inc) row (RS) K1, *kf&b; rep from * to last st, k1—570 sts. Work 12 rows in St st. Knit 2 rows. Bind off on WS knitwise.

FINISHING
Weave in ends. Arrange the ruffle folds and pin them to hold their shape while blocking. Block lightly. ●

2 Shawlette

KNITTED MEASUREMENTS
Width 51"/130cm
Length 19¾"/50cm

MATERIALS
- 6 1¾oz/50g balls (each approx 120yd/110m) of Classic Elite Yarns *Magnolia* (merino/silk) in #5449 sapphire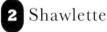
- One size 6 (4mm) circular needle, 40"/100cm long, OR SIZE TO OBTAIN GAUGE.
- Cable needle (cn)
- Stitch markers

GAUGE
22 sts and 32 rows = 4"/10cm over St st.
TAKE TIME TO CHECK GAUGE.

NOTE
Shawlette is knitted back and forth on circular needles from the top down.

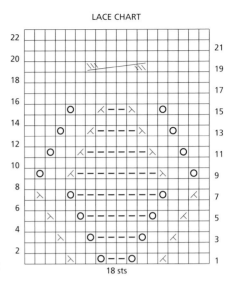

LACE CHART

18 sts

Stitch Key

☐ K on RS, p on WS	◹ K2tog
▬ P on RS, k on WS	◸ Ssk
Ⓞ Yo	6-st RC

GAUGE

22 sts and 32 rows = 4"/10cm over St st.
TAKE TIME TO CHECK GAUGE.

STITCH GLOSSARY

kf&b Knit into the front and back of st.
6-st RC Sl 3 sts to cn and hold in back,
k3, k3 from cn.

COAT SCARF

Cast on 28 sts. Knit 4 rows.
Row 1 (RS) K5, place marker (pm), work
row 1 of chart over next 18 sts, pm, k5.
Row 2 (WS) K5, slip marker (sm), work
row 2 of chart, sm, k5.
Cont as established through row 22 of
chart, then rep rows 1–22 thirteen times
more.
*Next (buttonhole) row (RS)** K5, sm,
work 19 sts of chart, sm, k2, yo, k2tog,
k1. Work 15 rows in pat as est. Repeat
from * once more, then work one more
buttonhole row.
Cont in pat until 16 repeats of chart are
completed, then work rows 1–15 of
chart once more. Remove markers while
working last row. Knit 3 rows.
Bind off purlwise.

RUFFLED EDGE

With circular needle and RS facing, pick
up and knit 258 sts from inner edge of
scarf (buttonhole edge). Purl 1 row.
Next (inc) row (RS) K1, *kf&b; repeat
from * to last st, k1—514 sts.
Work in St st for 10 rows. Knit 2 rows.
Bind off on WS knitwise.

FINISHING

Weave in all ends. Arrange the ruffle
folds and pin them to hold their
shape while blocking. Block lightly.
With RS facing, sew first button
6½"/16.5cm up from bottom edge to
left-hand garter st band, then sew
remaining 2 buttons at 2"/5cm
intervals above. ●

LACE CHART

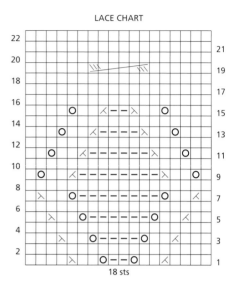

18 sts

Stitch Key

☐	K on RS, p on WS	◩	K2tog
⊟	P on RS, k on WS	◪	Ssk
Ⓞ	Yo	⧄⧄⧄	6-st RC

3 Coat Scarf

KNITTED MEASUREMENTS

Width 6½"/16.5cm
Length 47"/119cm

MATERIALS

- 4 1¾oz/50g balls (each approx
  120yd/110m) of Classic Elite Yarns
  Magnolia (merino/silk) in
  #5456 plum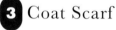
- One pair size 6 (4mm) needles OR
  SIZE TO OBTAIN GAUGE
- One size 6 (4mm) circular needle,
  40"/100cm long
- Cable needle (cn)
- Three ¾"/19mm buttons
- Stitch markers

•Pretty in Pink

By playing with yarn weight and varying the use of the swirl-stitch pattern, CAROL SULCOSKI creates three very different but equally lovely pink wraps.

1 A single repeat of the swirl stitch pattern becomes a delicate border in this ethereal SWIRL-EDGED STOLE.

2 This easy-to-knit SINGLE-REPEAT SCARF is worked in chunky *Toboggan* in a sweet ballerina pink.

3 Garter stitch edgings frame this MULTIPLE-REPEAT SCARF knit in luscious *Inca Alpaca*. The medium-weight yarn creates a scarf that will carry you through multiple seasons.

1/2

1 Swirl-Edged Stole

KNITTED MEASUREMENTS
Width 28"/71cm
Length 70"/172cm Long

MATERIALS
- 3 1¾oz/50g balls (each approx 440yd/402m) of Classic Elite Yarns *Silky Alpaca Lace* (alpaca/silk) in #2471 pixie pink (1)
- One size 7 (4.5mm) circular needle, 24"/60cm or longer, OR SIZE TO OBTAIN GAUGE
- Stitch markers

GAUGE
18 sts and 24 rows = 4"/10cm over St st. TAKE TIME TO CHECK GAUGE.

SWIRL STITCH
(Over multiple of 16 sts)
Row 1 (RS) Knit.
Row 2 and all WS rows Purl.
Rows 3, 5, 7, 9, and 11 K3, ssk, k2tog, k4, yo, k1, yo, k4.
Row 13 Knit.
Rows 15, 17, 19, 21, and 23 K4, yo, k1, yo, k4, ssk, k2tog, k3.
Row 24 Purl.
Repeat rows 1–24 for swirl st.

STOLE
Cast on 127 sts. Knit 10 rows.
Beg pats (RS) Work 5 sts in garter st (knit every row), work swirl st over next 16 sts, place marker (pm), work St st over next 85 sts, pm, work swirl st over next 16 sts, work garter st over rem 5 sts. Work in pats as est working rows 1–24 of swirl st 16 times, then work rows 1–12 once. Knit 10 rows. Bind off knitwise.

FINISHING
Weave in ends. Lightly block to measurements. ●

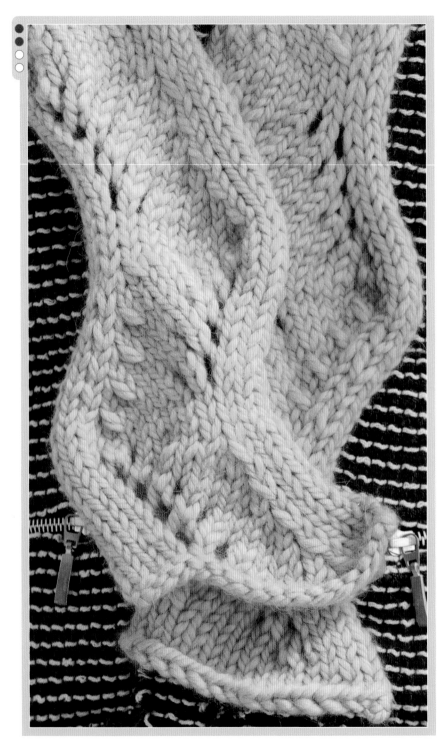

2 Single-Repeat Scarf

KNITTED MEASUREMENTS
Width 4"/10cm
Length 65"/165cm

MATERIALS
- 2 3½oz/100g hanks (each approx 87yd/80m) of Classic Elite Yarns *Toboggan* (merino/superfine alpaca) in #6719 ballerina pink (**5**)
- One pair size 10.5 (6.5mm) needles OR SIZE TO OBTAIN GAUGE

GAUGE
16 sts and 16 rows = 4"/10cm over swirl stitch.
TAKE TIME TO CHECK GAUGE.

SWIRL STITCH
Row 1 (RS) Knit.
Row 2 and all WS rows Purl.
Rows 3, 5, 7, 9, and 11 K3, ssk, k2tog, k4, yo, k1, yo, k4.
Row 13 Knit.
Rows 15, 17, 19, 21, and 23 K4, yo, k1, yo, k4, ssk, k2tog, k3.
Row 24 Purl.
Repeat rows 1–24 for swirl st.

SCARF
Cast on 16 sts. Work rows 1–24 of swirl st 10 times, then work rows 1–12 once. Bind off knitwise.

FINISHING
Weave in ends. Lightly block to measurements. ●

3 Multiple-Repeat Scarf

KNITTED MEASUREMENTS
Width 10"/25.5cm
Length 50"/127cm

MATERIALS
- 4 1¾oz/50g hanks (each approx 109yd/100m) of Classic Elite Yarns *Inca Alpaca* (baby alpaca) in #1148 rose (4)
- One pair size 7 (4.5mm) needles OR SIZE TO OBTAIN GAUGE

GAUGE
20 sts and 24 rows = 4"/10cm over swirl stitch.
TAKE TIME TO CHECK GAUGE.

SWIRL STITCH
Row 1 (RS) Knit.
Row 2 and all WS rows K5, p to last 5 sts, k5.
Rows 3, 5, 7, 9, and 11 K6, *k2, ssk, k2tog, k4, yo, k1, yo, k1; rep from * to last 8 sts, k8.
Row 13 Knit.
Rows 15, 17, 19, 21, and 23 K6, *k3, yo, k1, yo, k4, ssk, k2tog; rep from * to last 8 sts, k8.
Row 24 K5, p to last 5 sts, k5.
Repeat rows 1–24 for swirl st.

SCARF
Cast on 50 sts. Knit 8 rows. Work rows 1–24 of swirl st 12 times. Knit 8 rows. Bind off knitwise.

FINISHING
Weave in ends. Lightly block to measurements. ●

•Block Party

LINDA MEDINA works *Soft Linen*, a supple blend of linen, wool, and alpaca, in block and garter stitch to create three versatile pieces.

1 The wrap portion of this ASYMMETRICAL SHRUG is knit back and forth, then the single sleeve is worked in the round. In bright green, it s a fun and easy-to-wear look.

2 Knit in deep teal, a BLOCK AND GARTER SCARF makes a stunning addition to any outfit.

3 A cyan COWLNECK CAPELET is knit in the round for an easy finish. The collar can be worn up or folded down for different styling possibilities.

- Cable needle (cn)
- Stitch marker

GAUGE
24 sts and 32 rows/rnds to 4"/10cm over chart worked both in rows and in the rnd, using size 6 (4mm) needles. TAKE TIME TO CHECK GAUGE.

STITCH GLOSSARY
4-st slipped cross Sl next 3 sts to cn and hold at back, k next sl st, then return the last 2 knit sts from the cn to the LH needle, bring the cn to the front, k2 from the LH needle, then k sl st from the cn.

SHRUG
With straight needles, cast on 82 (98) sts.

GARTER STITCH BAND
Knit 5 rows. Purl 1 row on WS.

BEG CHART PAT IN ROWS
Row 1 (RS) Work to rep line, work 8-st rep 9 (11) times across, work to end of chart. Cont to follow chart until piece measures approx 54½"/138cm, end with row 2.

BLOCK & GARTER CHART (ROWS)

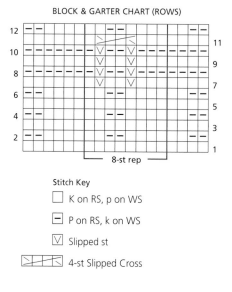

Stitch Key
- ☐ K on RS, p on WS
- ⊟ P on RS, k on WS
- ☑ Slipped st
- 4-st Slipped Cross

SLEEVE
Change to circular needle and begin to work from chart in rnds.
Rnd 3 (joining) Ssk, work to last 2 sts, k2tog, join and pm for beg of rnd—80 (96) sts. Slip marker each rnd. Work 6 rnds even.
Rnd 10 (dec) P2tog, work to last 2 sts, p2tog—78 (94) sts. Cont to work dec rnd every 7th (6th) rnd 15 (19) times more, working decs in pattern and changing to dpns when necessary—48 (56) sts. Work even until sleeve measures approx 15¼ (16¼)"/38 (41)cm from joining, end with a row 2, 4, or 6.

GARTER STITCH BAND
Rnds 1, 3, and 5 Knit.
Rnds 2 and 4 Purl.
Bind off purlwise. ●

BLOCK & GARTER CHART (RNDS)

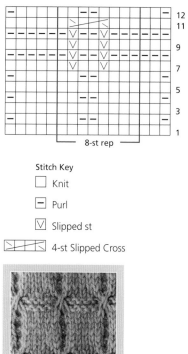

Stitch Key
- ☐ Knit
- ⊟ Purl
- ☑ Slipped st
- 4-st Slipped Cross

---

1 Asymmetrical Shrug

SIZES
Shrug is sized for Small/Medium (Large/X-Large); shown in size Small/Medium.

KNITTED MEASUREMENTS
Shrug length 54½"/138cm
Sleeve length 15¾ (16¾)"/40 (42.5)cm
Total length 70¼ (71¼)"/178 (180)cm
Shrug width and upper arm 13½ (16½)"/34 (42)cm
Sleeve cuff 8 (9)"/20.5 (23)cm

MATERIALS
- 6 (8) 1 3¾oz/50g balls (each 137yd/125m) of Classic Elite Yarns *Soft Linen* (linen/wool/baby alpaca) in #2281 new fern ③
- One pair size 6 (4mm) needles OR SIZE TO OBTAIN GAUGE
- One size 6 (4mm) circular needle, 16"/40cm long
- One set (5) size 6 (4mm) double-pointed needles (dpns)

BLOCK & GARTER CHART (ROWS)

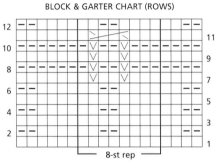

8-st rep

Stitch Key

☐ K on RS, p on WS

⊟ P on RS, k on WS

∨ Slipped st

◿◺ 4-st Slipped Cross

② Block & Garter Scarf

KNITTED MEASUREMENTS
Length approx 51"/129.5cm
Width 5.5"/14cm

MATERIALS
- 3 1¾oz/50g balls (each 137yd/125m) of Classic Elite Yarns *Soft Linen* (linen/wool/baby alpaca) in #2246 persian teal (⬛³)
- One pair size 6 (4mm) needles OR SIZE TO OBTAIN GAUGE
- Cable needle (cn)

GAUGE
24 sts and 32 rows to 4"/10cm over block and garter chart in rows using size 6 (4mm) needles.
TAKE TIME TO CHECK GAUGE.

STITCH GLOSSARY
4-st slipped cross Sl next 3 sts to cn and hold at back, k next sl st, then return the last 2 knit sts from the cn to the LH needle, bring the cn to the front, k2 from the LH needle, then k sl st from the cn.

SCARF
Cast on 34 sts.
Knit 5 rows.
Purl 1 row on WS.

BEG CHART PAT
Row 1 (RS) Work to rep line, work 8-st rep 3 times across, work to end of chart. Cont to follow chart until 12-row rep has been worked 33 times, work rows 1–6 once more. Knit 5 rows. Bind off.

FINISHING
Weave in ends. Block lightly to measurements. ●

 3 Cowlneck Capelet

SIZES
Capelet is sized for Small/Medium (Large/X-Large); shown in size Small/Medium.

KNITTED MEASUREMENTS
Length (without collar) approx
12½ (14)"/32 (35.5)cm
Circumference around lower edge
45 (50)"/114 (127)cm

MATERIALS
- 4 (6) 1¾oz/50g balls (each 137yd/125m) of Classic Elite Yarns *Soft Linen* (linen/wool/baby alpaca) in #2231 cyan (**3**)
- One each size 6 (4mm) circular needle, 16"/40cm and 24"/60cm long, OR SIZE TO OBTAIN GAUGE
- Cable needle (cn)
- Stitch marker

GAUGE
24 sts and 32 rnds to 4"/10cm over block and garter chart in the rnd using size 6 (4mm) needles.
TAKE TIME TO CHECK GAUGE.

STITCH GLOSSARY
4-st slipped cross Sl next 3 sts to cn and hold at back, k next sl st, then return the last 2 knit sts from the cn to the LH needle, bring the cn to the front, k2 from the LH needle, then k sl st from the cn.

GARTER STITCH BAND
Rnds 1, 3, and 5 Knit.
Rnds 2 and 4 Purl.
Rep rnds 1–5 for garter st band.

CAPELET
With longer circular needle, cast on 272 (304) sts. Place marker for beg of round and join, taking care not to twist sts. Sl marker on each round.

BEG CHART PAT
Rnd 1 Work to rep line, work 8-st rep 16 (18) times across, work to end of chart, pm for side edge, work to rep line, work 8-st rep 16 (18) times across, work to end of chart. Cont to follow chart until rnd 8 is complete.
Rnd 9 (dec) [Ssk, work chart to 2 sts before marker, k2tog] twice—268 (300) sts. Work 2 rnds even.
Rnd 12 (dec) [P2tog, work chart to 2 sts before marker, p2tog] twice—264 (296) sts. Cont to foll chart and rep dec rnd every third rnd 22 (26) times more, working decs in pattern and changing to shorter circular needle when necessary—176 (192) sts.
Work even until piece measures 12½ (14)"/32 (35.5)cm from beg, ending with any rnd 1–6.

FINISHING
Next rnd [K 20 (22), k2tog] 8 times around—168 (184) sts.

COWLNECK COLLAR
Next rnd [K2, p2] 42 (46) times around. Work even until ribbing measures 5"/12.5cm. Bind off loosely in rib. Weave in ends. Block lightly to measurements. ●

BLOCK & GARTER CHART (RNDS)

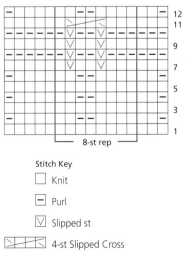

Stitch Key
- ☐ Knit
- ⊟ Purl
- ⩒ Slipped st
- 4-st Slipped Cross

• Power Cables

Cables have double the impact when knit in a reversible pattern. ANASTASIA BLAES makes use of three shades of pale blue and three different yarns to create maximum variety.

1 Spun from wool and nettles, *Woodland* is an unusual yarn that creates an uncommonly soft and wearable CABLED SCARF.

2 Garter stitch edgings frame the cable pattern in this cozy CABLED NECK WARMER knit in luscious merino *Ariosa*.

3 With its fiber combination of kid mohair, bamboo viscose, and nylon, *Pirouette* is the perfect yarn for a light and lacy CABLED WRAP.

GAUGES

20 sts and 30 rows = 4"/10cm
in St st using size 5 (3.75mm) needles

34½ sts and 29¼ rows = 4"/10cm
in reversible cable pat (after blocking)
using size 5 (3.75mm) needles.
TAKE TIME TO CHECK GAUGES.

STITCH GLOSSARY

s1p Slip one stitch purlwise.
8-st RC Sl 4 sts to cn and hold in
back, k1, p2, k1 from LH needle; k1,
p2, k1 from cn.
8-st LC Sl 4 sts to cn and hold in *front*,
k1, p2, k1 from LH needle; k1, p2, k1
from cn.

REVERSIBLE CABLE PATTERN

(44-st rep)
Row 1 [K1, p2, k2, p2] 3 times, k1, [k1,
p2, k2, p2] 3 times, k1.
Row 2 [P1, k2, p2, k2] 3 times, p1, [p1,
k2, p2, k2] 3 times, p1.
Rows 3 and 5 Rep row 1.
Rows 4 and 6 Rep row 2.
Row 7 (cable) 8-st RC, p2, k2, p2, 8-st
RC, 8-st LC, p2, k2, p2, 8-st LC.
Rows 8, 10, and 12 Rep row 2.
Rows 9 and 11 Rep row 1.
Row 13 (cable) K1, p2, k2, p2, 8-st RC,
[p2, k2] 3 times, p2, 8-st LC, p2,
k2, p2, k1.
Rows 14, 16, and 18 Rep row 2.
Rows 15 and 17 Rep row 1.
Row 19 (cable) 8-st LC, p2, k2, p2, 8-st
LC, 8-st RC, p2, k2, p2, 8-st RC.
Rows 20, 22, and 24 Rep row 2.
Rows 21 and 23 Rep row 1.
Row 25 (cable) K1, p2, k2, p2, 8-st LC,
[p2, k2] 3 times, p2, 8-st RC, p2,
k2, p2, k1.
Rep rows 2–25 for pat.

SCARF

Cast on 52 sts.
Row 1 S1p, p1, k1, p1, work row 1 of
cable pat, [p1, k1] twice.
Place stitch marker to mark for
odd-side rows.
Row 2 S1p, p1, k1, p1, work row 2 of
cable pat, [p1, k1] twice.
Rows 3–25 Cont in established pat,
working 4 sts each side of cable pat.
Rep rows 2–25 eighteen times more,
then rows 2–24 once.
Bind off all sts in pat.

FINISHING

Weave in ends. Block carefully to
measurements. ●

1 Cabled Scarf

KNITTED MEASUREMENTS

Width 6"/15cm (after blocking)
Length 66"/167.5cm (after blocking)

MATERIALS

- 4 1¾oz/50g balls (each approx.
  131yd/120m) of Classic Elite Yarns
  Woodland (wool/nettles) in #3192
  celestial (**3**)
- One pair size 5 (3.75mm) needles OR
  SIZE TO OBTAIN GAUGE
- Stitch marker (optional)
- Cable needle (cn)

GAUGES

15 sts and 22 rnds = 4"/10cm
in St st using size 10 (6mm) needle.

18 sts and 22 rnds = 4"/10cm
in cable pat using size 10 (6mm) needle
[after blocking].
TAKE TIME TO CHECK GAUGES.

STITCH GLOSSARY

8-st RC Sl 4 sts to cn and hold in
back, k1, p2, k1 from LH needle; k1,
p2, k1 from cn.
8-st LC Sl 4 sts to cn and hold in
front, k1, p2, k1 from LH needle; k1, p2,
k1 from cn.

NECK WARMER

Cast on 106 sts. Join, pm to indicate
beg of rnd and being careful not to
twist work.

BOTTOM EDGING

Rnds 1, 3, and 5 Knit.
Rnds 2 and 4 Purl.
Rnd 6 Purl, increasing 26 sts evenly
around—132 sts.

NECK

Rnd 1 *[K1, p2, k2, p2] 3 times, k1, rep
from * around.
Rnds 2–6 Rep rnd 1.
Rnd 7 (cable) *8-st RC, p2, k2, p2, 8-st
RC, 8-st LC, p2, k2, p2, 8-st LC, rep
from * around.
Rnds 8–12 Rep rnd 1.
Rnd 13 (cable) *K1, p2, k2, p2, 8-st RC,
(p2, k2) 3 times, p2, 8-st LC, p2, k2, p2,
k1, rep from * around.
Rnds 14–18 Rep rnd 1.
Rnd 19 (cable) *8-st LC, p2, k2, p2, 8-st
LC, 8-st RC, p2, k2, p2, 8-st RC, rep
from * around.
Rnds 20–24 Rep rnd 1.
Rnd 25 (cable) *K1, p2, k2, p2, 8-st LC,

(p2, k2) 3 times, p2, 8-st RC, p2, k2, p2,
k1, rep from * around.
Rep rnds 2–25 until work measures
approx 7 ½"/19cm from beg, ending
with rnd 19.

TOP EDGING

Rnd 1 Knit, decreasing 33 sts evenly
around—99 sts.
Rnd 2 Purl.
Rnd 3 Knit.
Rnd 4 Purl.
Bind off all sts knitwise.

FINISHING

Weave in ends. Block carefully to
measurements. ●

2 Cabled Neck Warmer

KNITTED MEASUREMENTS
Length 8"/20.5cm
Circumference 27"/68.5cm

MATERIALS
- 3 1¾oz/50g balls (each approx
  87yd/80m) of Classic Elite Yarns *Ariosa*
  (extrafine merino) in #4857
  ballad blue (5)
- One size 10 (6mm) circular needle,
  24"/61cm long OR SIZE TO
  OBTAIN GAUGE
- Stitch marker
- Cable needle (cn)

3 Cabled Wrap

KNITTED MEASUREMENTS
Length 70"/172cm
Width 14"/35.5cm (after blocking)

MATERIALS
- 3 0.9oz/25g balls (each approx. 246yd/225m) of Classic Elite Yarns *Pirouette* (kid mohair/bamboo viscose/nylon) in #4092 powder blue ❶
- One pair size 7 (4.5mm) needles OR SIZE TO OBTAIN GAUGE
- Stitch marker (optional)
- Cable needle (cn)

GAUGES
16 sts and 26 rows = 4"/10cm
in St st using size 7(4.5mm) needles.

22 sts and 24 rows = 4"/10cm
in reversible cable pat using size
7 (4.5mm) needles (after blocking).
TAKE TIME TO CHECK GAUGES.

STITCH GLOSSARY
s1p Slip one stitch purlwise.
8-st RC Sl 4 sts to cn and hold to back of work, k1, p2, k1 from LH needle; k1, p2, k1 from cn.
8-st LC Sl 4 sts to cn and hold to front of work, k1, p2, k1 from LH needle; k1, p2, k1 from cn.

REVERSIBLE CABLE PATTERN
(44-st rep)
Row 1 [K1, p2, k2, p2] 3 times, k1, [k1, p2, k2, p2] 3 times, k1.
Row 2 [P1, k2, p2, k2] 3 times, p1, [p1, k2, p2, k2] 3 times, p1.
Rows 3 and 5 Rep row 1.
Rows 4 and 6 Rep row 2.
Row 7 (cable) 8-st RC, p2, k2, p2, 8-st RC, 8-st LC, p2, k2, p2, 8-st LC.
Rows 8, 10, and 12 Rep row 2.
Rows 9 and 11 Rep row 1.
Row 13 (cable) K1, p2, k2, p2, 8-st RC, [p2, k2] 3 times, p2, 8-st LC, p2, k2, p2, k1.
Rows 14, 16, and 18 Rep row 2.
Rows 15 and 17 Rep row 1.
Row 19 (cable) 8-st LC, p2, k2, p2, 8-st LC, 8-st RC, p2, k2, p2, 8-st RC.
Rows 20, 22, and 24 Rep row 2.
Rows 21 and 23 Rep row 1.
Row 25 (cable) K1, p2, k2, p2, 8-st LC, [p2, k2] 3 times, p2, 8-st RC, p2, k2, p2, k1.
Rep rows 2–25 for pat.

WRAP
Cast on 92 sts loosely.
Row 1 S1p, p1, work row 1 of cable pat twice, p1, k1.
Place stitch marker to mark for odd-side rows.
Row 2 S1p, p1, work row 2 of cable pat twice, p1, k1.
Rows 3–25 Cont in established pat, working 2 sts each side of cable pat. Rep rows 2–25 sixteen times more, then rows 2–24 once.
Bind off all sts loosely in pat.

FINISHING
Weave in ends. Block carefully to measurements. ●

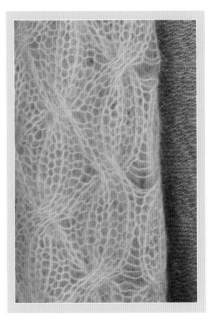

•Daisy Chain

CAROLYN NOYES creates a garden's worth of pretty scarves in *Alpaca Sox* kettle-dyed colors. Knit in shades of purple and featuring a daisy chain stitch motif, they're as fresh and lovely as a spring morning.

1 Worked along the long edge, this clever KEYHOLE SCARF features an opening to pull the opposite end through for wearing ease. Daisy stitch edgings give it feminine flair.

2 A jaunty JABOT is the perfect finishing touch to lift your spirits and brighten your look. Knit in a luscious shade of grape, this sweet adornment features a stockinette stitch body bookended with daisy stitch and bordered in garter stitch.

3 It's easy to customize the length of this PATCHWORK SCARF by varying the number of squares. One skein of *Alpaca Sox* is all you need to create a medium-length scarf; for a more dramatic look, add a second skein.

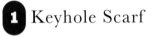

1 Keyhole Scarf

KNITTED MEASUREMENTS
Width 9"/23cm
Length 52"/132cm

MATERIALS
- 1 3½oz/100g hank (each approx 450yd/411m) of Classic Elite Yarns *Alpaca Sox* (alpaca/merino/nylon) in #1869 amethyst ①
- One size 5 (3.75mm) circular needle, 29"/73.5cm long, OR SIZE TO OBTAIN GAUGE
- Stitch markers

GAUGES
6 sts and 5 rows = 1"/2.5cm over daisy chain pat using size 5 (3.75mm) needles.

24 sts and 32 rows = 4"/10cm over St st using size 5 (3.75mm) needles.
TAKE TIME TO CHECK GAUGES.

STITCH GLOSSARY
Cluster stitch Wyif, [sl next st, dropping extra 2 yarnovers] 5 times; [bring yarn to back between needles, sl 5 sts back to left needle, bring yarn to front between needles, sl 5 sts to right needle] twice.

W&T (Wrap & Turn)
Knit the number of stitches indicated, slip next stitch purlwise, bring yarn to front of work, return slipped stitch back to left needle, turn work, continue row as instructed—one stitch wrapped.

SCARF
Cast on 269 sts, pm after first 8 sts and before last 8 sts.
Row 1 Knit.
Work short row on garter edge: K7, W&T; turn work, k6, sl 1 wyif.
Next row (WS) Knit to last st, sl 1 wyif.
Next row (RS) K7, k1 pluswrap; slip marker, work row 2 of daisy chain chart to next marker, slip marker, k7, sl 1 wyif.
Work short row on garter edge: K7, W&T; turn work, k6, sl 1 wyif.
Next row (WS) K7, k1 pluswrap; slip marker, work row 3 of daisy chain chart to next marker, slip marker, k7, sl 1 wyif.
Note: Instructions now refer to stitches between markers only; keep edge stitches in garter st (knit all rows) throughout. Slip last st of each row wyif.
Work rows 4 and 5 of daisy chain chart. Work in St st for 3"/7.5cm, ending with a RS row.

Next row (WS) P192, k19, purl to marker.
Divide for keyhole: K42, bind off 19 sts, k192 to marker.
Next row (WS) P192, pm, cast on 19 sts, pm, p42.
Next row (RS) Knit.
Next 5 rows Cont as established, working 19 sts between keyhole markers in daisy chain chart pat.
Next row (RS) Cont as established, binding off 19 sts between keyhole markers.
Next row Cont as established, casting on 19 sts between keyhole markers.
Next row Cont as established to keyhole marker, purl to next keyhole marker, cont as established to end.
Next row Purl, removing keyhole markers. Work in St st for 3"/7.5cm, ending with a RS row. Work rows 1–3 of daisy chain chart.
Note Rows include edge stitches once more. Work short row on garter edge: K7, W&T, k6, sl 1 wyif.
Next row (RS) K7, k1 pluswrap; remove marker, knit to last st, sl 1 wyif.
Work short row on garter edge: K7, W&T, k6, sl 1 wyif.
Next row (WS) K7, k1 pluswrap; remove marker, knit to last st, sl 1 wyif. Bind off.

FINISHING
Weave in ends. Block to measurements. ●

DAISY CHAIN CHART

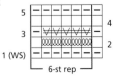

Stitch Key

☐ K on RS, p on WS

⊟ K on WS

▨ K1, wrapping yarn 3 times around needle (instead of once)

Cluster stitch

2 Jabot

KNITTED MEASUREMENTS
Width at midsection 5"/13cm
Length 44½"/113cm

MATERIALS
- 1 3½oz/100g hank (each approx 450yd/411m) of Classic Elite Yarns *Alpaca Sox* (alpaca/merino/nylon) in #1826 pansy (**1**)
- One pair size 5 (3.75mm) needles OR SIZE TO OBTAIN GAUGE
- Stitch markers

GAUGES
6 sts and 5 rows = 1"/2.5cm over daisy chain pat using size 5 (3.75mm) needles.

24 sts and 32 rows = 4"/10cm over stockinette st using size 5 (3.75mm) needles.
TAKE TIME TO CHECK GAUGES.

STITCH GLOSSARY
Cluster stitch Wyif, [sl next st, dropping extra 2 yarnovers] 5 times; [bring yarn to back between needles, sl 5 sts back to left needle, bring yarn to front between needles, sl 5 sts to right needle] twice.

NOTE
Slip the first stitch of each row purlwise.

JABOT
Cast on 45 sts, pm after first 4 sts and before last 4 sts. Instructions refer to stitches between markers only, keep edge stitches in garter st (knit all rows) throughout.
Row 1 (RS) Knit.
Rows 2–6 Work daisy chain chart over center 37 sts (starting with a WS row), keeping edge sts in garter st as established.
Rows 7–15 Work in St st.
Row 16 (WS) Work row 1 of daisy chain chart.
Row 17 K4, work row 2 of daisy chain chart as follows: Work the 6-st rep 5 times, k3.
Row 18 K3, work row 3 of daisy chain chart as follows: Work the 6-st rep 5 times, k4.
Rows 19–20 Work rows 4 and 5 of daisy chain chart.
Rows 21–29 Work in St st.
Rows 30–40 Rep rows 2–12.
Row 41 (dec) (RS) After first marker, [ssk] twice, knit to 4 sts before second marker, [k2tog] twice—33 sts between markers.
Row 42 Purl.
Row 43 (dec) (RS) After first marker, ssk, knit to 2 sts before second marker, k2tog—31 sts between markers. Work daisy chain chart for 5 rows. Work in St st for 8 rows.
Next (dec) row (RS) Rep row 41—27 sts between markers. Work in St st for 17 rows.

Next (dec) row (RS) Rep row 41—23 sts between markers. Work even in St st for 23"/58.5cm, ending with a WS row.
Next (inc) row (RS) After first marker, [M1] twice, knit to second marker, [M1] twice—27 sts between markers. Work in St st for 17 rows.
Next (inc) row (RS) Rep last inc row—31 sts between markers. Work in St st for 8 rows. Work daisy chain chart for 5 rows.
Next (inc) row (RS) After first marker, M1, knit to second marker, M1—33 sts between markers. Purl 1 row.
Next (inc) row (RS) After first marker, [M1] twice, knit to second marker, [M1] twice—37 sts between markers. Work in St st for 4 rows. Work daisy chain chart for 5 rows. Work in St st for 7 rows, ending with a RS row.
Next 5 rows Rep rows 16–20 from beg of jabot. Work in St st for 9 rows, ending with a RS row. Work daisy chain chart for 5 rows.
Next row (RS) Knit. Bind off.

FINISHING
Weave in ends. Block to measurements. ●

DAISY CHAIN CHART

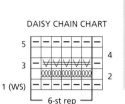

6-st rep

Stitch Key

- ☐ K on RS, p on WS
- ⊟ K on WS
- ▨ K1, wrapping yarn 3 times around needle (instead of once)
- ⩔⩔⩔⩔ Cluster stitch

❸ Patchwork Scarf

SIZES
Instructions are written for two lengths: 54"/137cm and 72"/183cm; 72"/183cm-long scarf shown.

KNITTED MEASUREMENTS
Width 9"/23cm
Length 54 (72)"/137 (183)cm

MATERIALS
- 1 (2) 3½oz/100g hank (each approx 450yd/411m) of Classic Elite Yarns *Alpaca Sox* (alpaca/merino /nylon) in #1852 viola ❶
- One pair size 5 (3.75mm) needles OR SIZE TO OBTAIN GAUGE
- Stitch markers

GAUGES
6 sts and 5 rows = 1"/2.5cm over daisy chain pat using size 5 (3.75mm) needles.

24 sts and 32 rows = 4"/10cm over stockinette st using size 5 (3.75mm) needles.
TAKE TIME TO CHECK GAUGES.

STITCH GLOSSARY
Cluster stitch Wyif, [sl next st, dropping extra 2 yarnovers] 5 times; [bring yarn to back between needles, sl 5 sts back to left needle, bring yarn to front between needles, sl 5 sts to right needle] twice.

K1, P1 RIB
(over a multiple of 2 sts plus 1)
Row 1 (RS) *K1, p1; rep from * to last st; k1.
Row 2 K the knit sts and p the purl sts.
Rep row 2 for k1, p1 rib.

NOTES
When measuring swatch for gauge, row count is important to ensure that each square will block out square. If you are getting gauge for stitches but not for rows, work more/fewer rows in the stockinette sections to reach the correct measurements in the instructions.

SQUARE
(make 6 for 54"/137cm scarf; 8 for 72"/183cm scarf)
Cast on 55 sts, pm after first 3 and before last 3 sts. Instructions refer to stitches between markers only; keep edge stitches in garter st (knit all rows) throughout.
Rows 1 (RS) and 2 Work in k1, p1 rib.
Rows 3–7 Work in St st.
Work daisy chain chart over center 49 sts (starting with a WS row), keeping edge sts in garter st as established, for 5 rows. Work in St st for 15 rows. Rep last 20 rows once.
Work 5 rows of chart. Work in St st for 5 rows, ending with a RS row. Work k1, p1 rib for 2 rows. Bind off.

FINISHING
Lightly block each square to 9"/23cm square. Sew squares tog, alternating direction of daisy chain pat. ●

•Shades of Gray

HOLLI YEOH explores the possibilities of a single stitch pattern in her trio of fern-stitch scarves. By keeping the color family, basic design, and stitch pattern the same and varying just the yarn, she creates something for everyone.

1 Wool and alpaca *MountainTop Vista* creates a WORSTED WEIGHT SCARF perfect for fall. In ash-gray, it will complement any color of coat.

2 This LACEWEIGHT SCARF knit in baby alpaca and bamboo viscose *MountainTop Vail* makes a lovely, light cover-up for a cool evening.

3 This CHUNKY SCARF is knit in *MountainTop Blackthorn*, a sumptuous blend of wool and alpaca. Slip it on when the temperatures start to dip.

(4mm) needles.
TAKE TIME TO CHECK GAUGE.

STITCH GLOSSARY

Inc3 Into the same stitch, k1, yo, k1, for a total of 3 sts in one st.
LRI (left-slanting raised increase) With LH needle, pick up st in row directly below last st worked and knit into the back of it.
RRI (right-slanting raised increase) With RH needle, knit into st in row directly below the next st on LH needle.

SCARF

With smaller needles, cast on 43 sts.
Row 1 Sl 1 purlwise, knit to end of row. Rep last row 7 times more. Change to larger needles. Beg with row 1 of Fern Stitch Chart I (page 54), work first 10 sts, work 12-st rep 2 times, work last 9 sts. Cont to foll chart in this way to row 20, then rep rows 1–20 eighteen times more. Change to smaller needles.
Next row (RS) Sl 1 purlwise, knit to end of row. Rep last row 5 times more. Bind off.

FINISHING

Weave in ends.
Block to measurements. ●

① Worsted Weight Scarf

KNITTED MEASUREMENTS
Width approx 7"/18cm
Length approx 58"/147cm

MATERIALS
● 4 1¾oz/50g hanks (each approx 100yd/91m) of Classic Elite Yarns *MountainTop Vista* (wool/superfine alpaca) in #6006 wolf (■4■)
● One pair size 6 (4mm) needles OR SIZE TO OBTAIN GAUGE
● One pair size 4 (3.5mm) needles

GAUGE
24 sts and 27 rows to 4"/10cm over stitch pat using size 6

TAKE TIME TO CHECK GAUGE.

STITCH GLOSSARY

Inc3 Into the same stitch, k1, yo, k1, for a total of 3 sts in one st.
LRI (left-slanting raised increase) With LH needle, pick up st in row directly below last st worked and knit into the back of it.
RRI (right-slanting raised increase) With RH needle, knit into st in row directly below the next st on LH needle.

NOTE

Knitted measurements and gauge refer to relaxed size after aggressive blocking.

SCARF

With smaller needles, cast on 43 sts.
Row 1 Sl 1 purlwise, knit to end of row.
Rep last row 7 times more.
Change to larger needles.
*Beg with row 1 of Fern Stitch Chart I (page 154), work first 10 sts, work 12-st rep 2 times, work last 9 sts.
Cont to foll chart in this way to row 20, then rep rows 1–10. Rep from * 13 times more. Change to smaller needles.
Next row (RS) Sl 1 purlwise, knit to end of row. Rep last row 5 times more. Bind off.

FINISHING

Weave in ends. Block aggressively to approx 9"/22.5cm x 65"/165cm. When dry, piece will relax to finished measurements. ●

② Laceweight Scarf

KNITTED MEASUREMENTS
Width approx 7½"/19cm
Length approx 60"/152cm

MATERIALS
● 2 1¾oz/50g hanks (each approx 236yd/215m) of Classic Elite Yarns *MountainTop Vail* (baby alpaca/bamboo viscose) in #6403 steel ①
● One pair size 5 (3.75mm) needles OR SIZE TO OBTAIN GAUGE
● One pair size 4 (3.5mm) needles

GAUGE
23 sts and 28 rows to 4"/10cm over stitch pat using size 5 (3.75mm) needles.

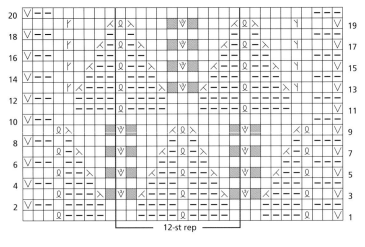

12-st rep

FERN STITCH CHART II

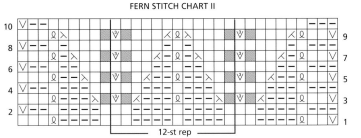

12-st rep

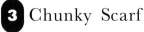

③ Chunky Scarf

KNITTED MEASUREMENTS
Width approx 8½"/21.5cm
Length approx 65"/165cm

MATERIALS
- 3 3½oz/100g hanks (each approx 120yd/110m) of Classic Elite Yarns *MountainTop Blackthorn* (wool/superfine alpaca) in #7077 seal
- One pair size 11 (8mm) needles OR SIZE TO OBTAIN GAUGE
- One pair size 10½ (6.5mm) needles

GAUGE
14 sts and 17 rows to 4"/10cm over stitch pat using size 11 (8mm) needles
TAKE TIME TO CHECK GAUGE.

STITCH GLOSSARY
Inc3 Into the same stitch, k1, yo, k1, for a total of 3 sts in one st.
LRI (left-slanting raised increase)
With LH needle, pick up st in row directly below last st worked and knit into the back of it.

RRI (right-slanting raised increase)
With RH needle, knit into st in row directly below the next st on LH needle.

SCARF
With smaller needles, cast on 31 sts.
Row 1 Sl 1 purlwise, knit to end of row.
Rep last row 5 times more. Change to larger needles.
Beg with row 1 of Fern Stitch Chart II, work first 10 sts, work 12-st rep once, work last 9 sts. Cont to foll chart in this way to row 10, then rep rows 1–10 twenty-six times more. Change to smaller needles.
Next row (RS) Sl 1 purlwise, knit to end of row. Rep last row 3 times more. Bind off.

FINISHING
Weave in ends. Block to measurements. ●

Stitch Key
☐	K on RS, p on WS
—	P on RS, k on WS
℧	K1tbl
∨	Sl 1 pwise
╱	K2tog
╲	Ssk
⎰	RR1
⎱	LR1
⊽	Inc 3
▨	No stitch

•Lacy Leaves

BROOKE NICO's mastery of lace knitting is apparent in these stunningly beautiful pieces that mix leaf lace and faggotted rib in various configurations.

1 This small, lightweight LEAF LACE RUFF in variegated *Silky Alpaca Lace* is perfect for the first days of autumn or spring.

2 The light triangle-shaped LEAF LACE SHAWL boasts an elegant leaf lace edging and insertion running down the back. Thistle-colored *Silky Alpaca Lace* makes it a fabulously feminine design.

3 Mohair *Gisele* makes this LEAF LACE SCARF lush and cozy. The double panel of leaves forms a subtle ruffle.

1 Leaf Lace Ruff

KNITTED MEASUREMENTS
Circumference 21"/53.5cm
Width 7"/18cm

MATERIALS
- 1 1¾oz/50g ball (each approx 440yd/402m) of Classic Elite Yarns *Silky Alpaca Lace* (alpaca/silk) in #2456 clover blossom ⓪
- One pair size 0 (2mm) needles OR SIZE TO OBTAIN GAUGE
- Stitch holder
- Waste yarn

GAUGE
34 sts and 32 rows = 4"/10cm
over Lace Chart pattern, after blocking
TAKE TIME TO CHECK GAUGE.

STITCH GLOSSARY
5 dec to 1 Knit until there are 5 sts on RH needle, pass the 2nd, 3rd, 4th, and 5th sts one at a time over the first st.

NOTE
Stitch count varies on each row of chart.

RUFF
Using waste yarn, cast on 65 sts. Work in St st for 3 rows. Change to working yarn.
Next row (WS) K7, p9, k33, p9, k7.
Est chart (RS) Beg Lace Chart and repeat rows 1–12 until piece measures 21"/53.5cm or desired circumference. Do not bind off. Place sts on holder. Cut yarn, leaving a 36"/91.5cm tail.

FINISHING
Lightly block to measurements. Place sts from holder onto needle. Remove waste yarn from cast-on edge and place these sts onto a second needle. Graft sts together. Weave in ends. ●

Stitch Key

□	K on RS, p on WS
−	P on RS, k on WS
O	Yo
⟋	K2tog on RS, ssk on WS
⟍	Ssk on RS, k2tog on WS
⅄	SK2P
⌒	Bind off
⟋⟍	5 dec to 1
▨	No stitch

LACE CHART

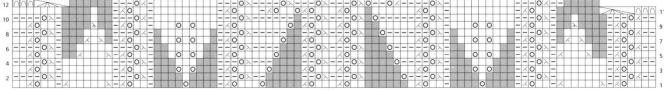

65 sts

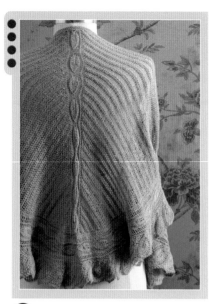

2 Leaf Lace Shawl

KNITTED MEASUREMENTS
Width 66"/167.5cm
Length 26"/66cm

MATERIALS
- 3 1¾oz/50g balls (each approx 440yd/402m) of Classic Elite Yarns *Silky Alpaca Lace* (alpaca/silk) in #2419 fandango pink) (0)
- One pair size 0 (2mm) needles OR SIZE TO OBTAIN GAUGE
- One size 0 (2mm) circular needle, 29"/75cm long
- Stitch markers

GAUGE
25 sts and 44 rows = 4"/10cm over faggoted rib pattern, after blocking.
TAKE TIME TO CHECK GAUGE.

STITCH GLOSSARY
5 dec to 1 Knit until there are 5 sts on RH needle, pass the 2nd, 3rd, 4th, and 5th sts one at a time over the first st.

FAGGOTED RIB PATTERN
(over a multiple of 4 sts)
All rows *K2, yo, k2tog; rep from *.

NOTE
Stitch count varies on each row of charts.

SHAWL
CENTER TOP TAB
Using straight needles, cast on 4 sts.
Work 32 rows in garter st (k every row).
Next row K4, turn piece slightly and pick up 16 sts along side of tab, pick up 4 sts along cast-on edge—24 sts.
Next row K4, place marker (pm), k4, pm, k8, pm, k4, pm, k4.

BEG CHART
Next row (RS) The 4 sts at the beg and end of each row are worked in garter st, faggoted rib pat is worked between markers 1 and 2 and between markers 3 and 4, and center 8 sts are worked in leaf pat. Beg Body Chart and work rows 1–24, increasing 4 sts each RS row as indicated on chart (by yo), and work these incs into faggoted rib pat as indicated by highlighted area of chart. (You may want to redistribute markers each time a full repeat of faggoted rib pat is added.) Rep rows 1–24 of chart a total of 8 times, changing to circular needle as needed—408 sts.
Next row (RS) Knit. Do not bind off and keep sts on circular needle; set aside.

EDGING
With straight needles, cast on 32 sts. Work set-up row (WS) of Edging Chart 1 to last st. With WS of body facing, work ssk over last st of edging with first st of body from circular needle. Cont in this manner, attaching edging to body by ssk at the end of every WS row. Complete rows 1–22 of Edging Chart 1. Beg Edging Chart 2 and repeat rows 1–24 a total of 32 times (12 body sts rem). Cont to Edging Chart 3 and work rows 1–24 once. Bind off.

FINISHING
Weave in ends. Lightly block to measurements. ●

2 Leaf Lace Shawl

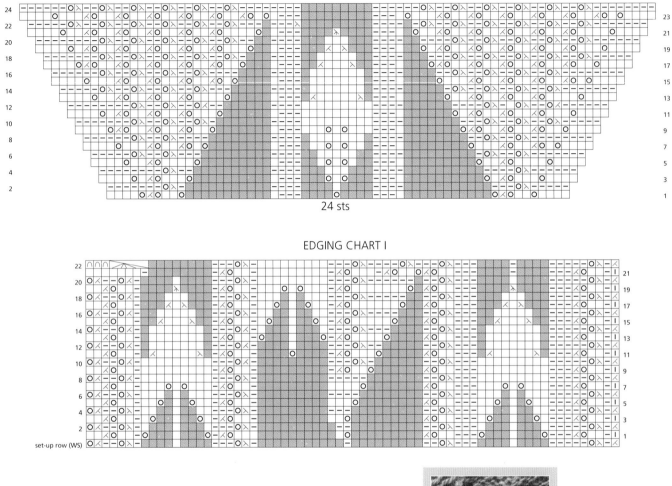

BODY CHART

24 sts

EDGING CHART I

set-up row (WS)

Stitch Key

- ☐ K on RS, p on WS
- ― P on RS, k on WS
- ☑ Yo
- ⟋ K2tog on RS, ssk on WS
- ⟍ Ssk on RS, k2tog on WS
- ⋏ SK2P
- ⌒ Bind off
- ☐ Sl1 wyif
- ⟍ Ssk last edge st with shawl body st
- ⟋⟍ 5 dec to 1
- ▨ No stitch
- ☐ Highlighted area is a guide to working increased sts into pattern

62

EDGING CHART 2

EDGING CHART 3

3 Leaf Lace Scarf

KNITTED MEASUREMENTS
Width 10"/25.5cm
Length 72"/182.5cm

MATERIALS
- 3 1¾oz/50g balls (each approx 230yd/210cm) of Classic Elite Yarns *Giselle* (kid mohair/wool/nylon) in #4120 darrow river (3)
- One pair size 7 (4.5mm) needles OR SIZE TO OBTAIN GAUGE

GAUGE
26 sts and 20 rows = 4"/10cm over Chart 2, after blocking.
TAKE TIME TO CHECK GAUGE.

STITCH GLOSSARY
5 dec to 1 Knit until there are 5 sts on RH needle, pass the 2nd, 3rd, 4th, and 5th sts one at a time over the first st.

NOTE
Stitch count varies on each row of charts.

SCARF
Cast on 35 sts.

BEG CHART
Next row (RS) Beg Chart 1 and work rows 1–12 once—65 sts.
Change to Chart 2 and rep rows 1–12 a total of 27 times. Change to Chart 3 and work rows 1–24 once—23 sts.
Bind off.

FINISHING
Weave in ends.
Lightly block to measurements. ●

CHART 1

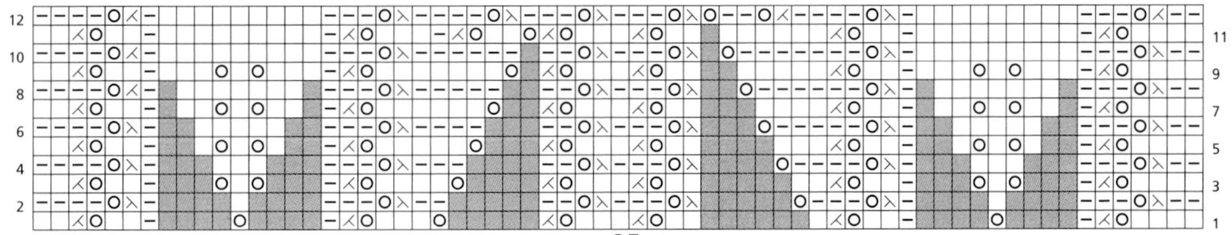

35 sts

CHART 2

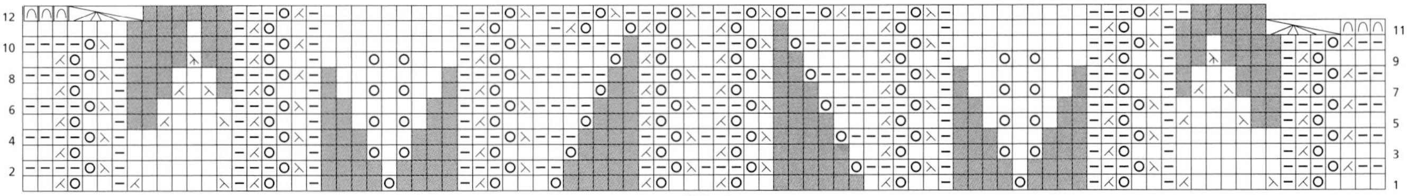

65 sts

CHART 3

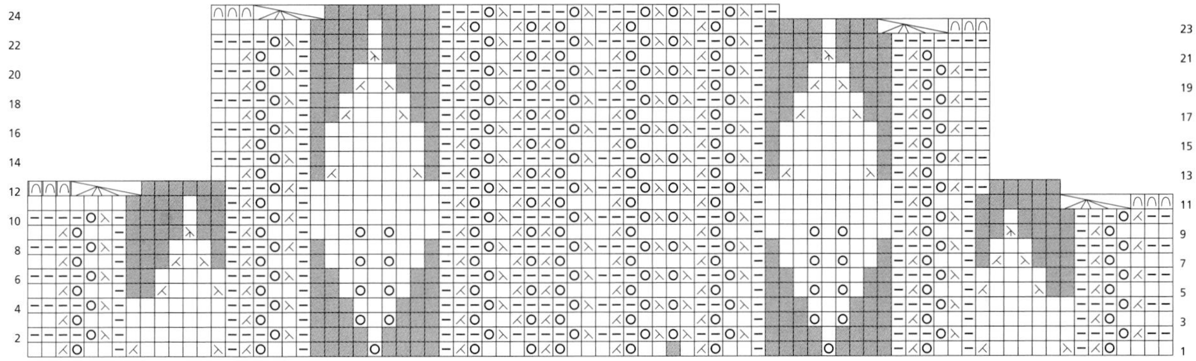

65 sts

Stitch Key

☐ K on RS, p on WS

─ P on RS, k on WS

◉ Yarn over

◿ K2tog on RS, ssk on WS

◺ Ssk on RS, k2tog on WS

◿ SK2P

⌒ Bind off

 5 dec to 1

▦ No stitch

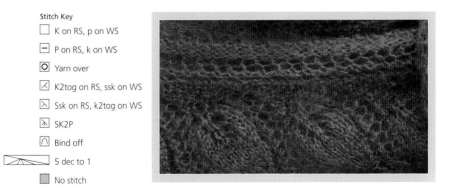

•Red Alert!

Fluffy, fabulous mohair takes center stage in ANASTASIA BLAES's trio of luscious red toppers. All three scrumptious designs feature a lovely leaf lace stitch pattern that shows off the light and airy fiber.

1 This lovely MOHAIR CAPELET is worked in worsted-weight mohair *La Gran* in deep merlot. It features an elegant lace insertion against stockinette and a garter stitch collar and hem.

2 This delicate MOHAIR SCARF knit in bright salmon red *Pirouette* will add a dash of elegance to any ensemble.

3 A dusty rose MOHAIR WRAP is the perfect evening cover-up when you need a touch of sizzle.

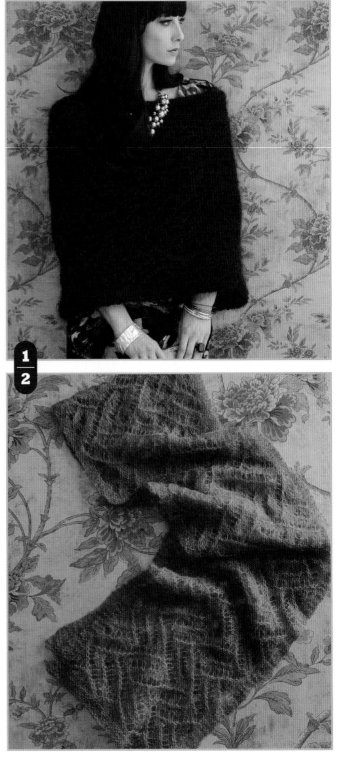

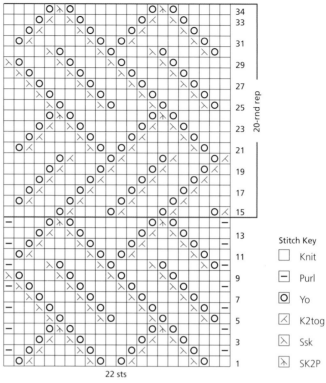

LACE CHART (CAPELET)

22 sts

20-rnd rep

Stitch Key

	Knit
−	Purl
O	Yo
⟋	K2tog
⟍	Ssk
⟑	SK2P

① Mohair Capelet

FINISHED MEASUREMENTS
Neck circumference 28"/71cm
Length 20½"/52cm (after blocking)

MATERIALS
- 3 1¾oz/50g balls (each approx 106yd/97m) of Classic Elite Yarns *La Gran* (mohair/wool/nylon) in #6555 infra red (**4**)
- One size 13 (9mm) circular needle, 29"/75cm long, OR SIZE TO OBTAIN GAUGE
- Stitch markers

GAUGE
10 sts and 15 rows = 4"/10cm
over St st using size 13 (9mm) needles.
TAKE TIME TO CHECK GAUGE.

NOTE
Capelet is worked in the round from the top down.

STITCH GLOSSARY
SK2P Slip 1, k2tog, pass the slipped st over the k2tog.

GARTER STITCH
(worked in the rnd)
Rnd 1 Knit.
Rnd 2 Purl.
Rep rnds 1–2 for garter st.

STOCKINETTE STITCH (St st)
(worked in the round)
Knit every round.

CAPELET
Cast on 68 sts. Place marker (pm) for beg of rnd and join, being careful not to twist sts. Work in garter st for 6 rnds.
Rnd 1 (inc) [K4, m1] twice, k1, pm, work rnd 1 of chart over next 22 sts, pm, k1, m1, [k4, m1] 9 times—80 sts.
Rnd 2 P to marker, work rnd 2 of chart, p to end.
Rnd 3 K to marker, work chart as est, k to end.
Rnd 4 P to marker, work chart as est, p to end.
Rnd 5 (inc) K4, m1, k5, m1, k2, work chart as est, k2, m1, [k5, m1] 9 times—92 sts.
Rnd 6 P to marker, work as est chart, p to end.

Rnd 7 K to marker, work chart as est, k to end.

Rnd 8 P to marker, work chart as est, p to end.

Rnd 9 (inc) K4, m1, k6, m1, k3, work chart as est, k3, m1, [k6, m1] 9 times—104 sts.

Rnd 10 P to marker, work as est chart, p to end.

Rnd 11 K to marker, work chart as est, k to end.

Rnd 12 P to marker, work chart as est, p to end.

Rnd 13 (inc) K4, m1, k7, m1, k4, work chart as est, k4, m1, [k7, m1] 9 times—116 sts.

Rnd 14 P to marker, work as est chart, p to end.

Rnd 15 K to marker, work chart as est, k to end.

Cont in St st and chart pat as est, repeating rnds 15–34 for pat. Work even until capelet measures approx. 19"/48cm from cast-on edge, ending with rnd 20 of chart. Work garter st for 6 rnds. Bind off.

FINISHING

Weave in ends. Block to measurements. ●

2 Mohair Scarf

KNITTED MEASUREMENTS
Width 10"/25cm
Length 65"/165cm (after blocking)

MATERIALS
● 2 0.9oz/25g balls (each approx 246yd/225m) of Classic Elite Yarns *Pirouette* (kid mohair/bamboo viscose/nylon) in #4088 electric salmon ①

● One pair size 8 (5mm) needles OR SIZE TO OBTAIN GAUGE

GAUGE
15 sts and 24 rows = 4"/10cm over chart pat (after blocking) using size 8 (5mm) needles.
TAKE TIME TO CHECK GAUGE.

STITCH GLOSSARY
ssp Slip 2 sts knitwise, return to LH needle, p2tog through back loops.
sssp Slip 3 sts knitwise, return to LH needle, p3tog through back loops.

SCARF
Cast on 38 sts. Knit 7 rows.
Next row (WS) K4, p30, k4.

BEG CHART PAT
Row 1 (RS) Work chart pat, repeating rows 1–20 until piece measures approx 64"/162.5cm from beg, ending with row 4 of chart. (Block lightly as you work for accurate measurements.)
Keeping 4 sts each side in garter st (k every row) as est, k 1 row, p 1 row, k 6 rows. Bind off.

FINISHING
Weave in ends. Block to measurements. ●

LACE CHART (SCARF)

38 sts

Stitch Key

☐ K on RS, p on WS

⊟ P on RS, k on WS

◯ Yo

⟋ K2tog on RS, p2tog on WS

⟍ Ssk on RS, ssp on WS

⋀ Sssp on WS

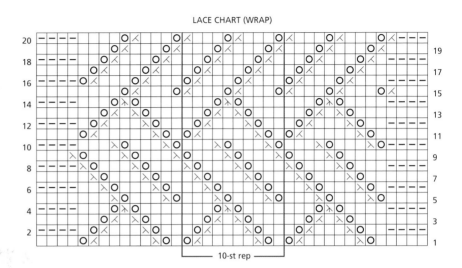

LACE CHART (WRAP)

⎯ 10-st rep ⎯

3 Mohair Wrap

KNITTED MEASUREMENTS
Width 23"/58cm
Length 52"/132cm (after blocking)

MATERIALS
- 2 1¾oz/50g balls (each approx 230yd/210m) of Classic Elite Yarns *Giselle* (kid mohair/wool/nylon) in #4188 cordoba rosa (⬛3)
- One size 9 (5.5mm) circular needle, 36"/91cm long, OR SIZE TO OBTAIN GAUGE

GAUGE
12 sts and 19 rows = 4"/10cm over chart pat (after blocking) using size 9 (91cm) needle.
TAKE TIME TO CHECK GAUGE.

STITCH GLOSSARY
ssp Slip 2 sts knitwise, return to LH needle, p2tog through back loops.
sssp Slip 3 sts knitwise, return to LH needle, p3tog through back loops.

Stitch Key
- ☐ K on RS, p on WS
- ⊟ P on RS, k on WS
- ⊡ Yo
- ⧄ K2tog on RS, p2tog on WS
- ⧅ Ssk on RS, ssp on WS
- ⧆ Sssp on WS

WRAP
Cast on 158 sts. Working back and forth on circular needle, knit 7 rows.
Next row (WS) K4, p to last 4 sts, k4.

BEG CHART PAT
Row 1 (RS) Work chart to rep line, work 10 st rep 13 times, work to end of chart. Repeat rows 1–20 of chart 4 times, then work rows 1–14 once. Keeping 4 sts each side in garter st (k every row) as est, k 1 row, p 1 row, k 6 rows. Bind off.

FINISHING
Weave in ends. Block to measurements. ●

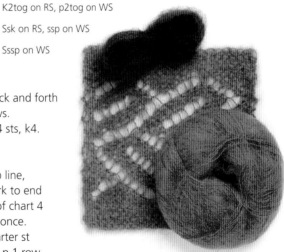

•Wrap Stars

JEAN MOSS frames bold blocks of color with black for three graphic looks. Each piece features a zigzag stitch pattern and bulky *Toboggan* yarn, with a different focal color and silhouette.

1 The leaf-green ZIGZAG WRAP is a simple rectangular shoulder warmer that closes with a single button that serves as a focal point.

2 You'll be ready for a night at the opera in this ZIGZAG CAPELET in garnet with a rhinestone closure.

3 The ZIGZAG COWL doubles up for extra warmth. The periwinkle color blocks really pop against the black accents.

1 Zigzag Wrap

KNITTED MEASUREMENTS
Length including edging 42"/106.5cm
Width including edging 7½"/19cm

MATERIALS
- 2 3½oz/100g hanks (each approx 87yd/80m) of Classic Elite Yarns *Toboggan* (merino wool/superfine alpaca) in #6715 leaf (MC) (6)
- 1 hank in #6713 ebony (CC)
- One pair size 15 (10mm) needles OR SIZE TO OBTAIN GAUGE
- Size 8/H (5mm) crochet hook
- One 1½"/4cm button

GAUGE
11 sts and 15 rows = 4"/10cm over zigzag pattern.
TAKE TIME TO CHECK GAUGE.

STITCH GLOSSARY
LT Knit into back of second st on LH needle without dropping st from LH needle, then knit first 2 sts on LH needle together through back loops. Drop both sts from LH needle.
RT K2tog but do not slip from needle. Insert RH needle between the sts just knitted tog and knit the first stitch again, then slip both stitches from the needle together.

ZIGZAG PATTERN
(over a multiple of 4 sts)
Rows 1, 3, 5, and 7 (WS) With MC, sl 1, p to last st, k1tbl.
Row 2 Sl 1, *LT, k2; rep from * to last 3 sts, LT, k1tbl.
Row 4 Sl 1, k1, *LT, k2; rep from * to last 2 sts, end k1, k1 tbl.
Row 6 S1, *k2, LT; rep from * to last 3 sts, k2, k1tbl.

Row 8 Sl 1, k1, *k2, LT; rep from * to last 2 sts, k1, k1tbl.
Rows 9–16 Rep rows 1–8.
Rows 17–20 With CC, purl.
Rows 21, 23, 25, and 27 (WS) With MC, sl 1, p to last st, k1tbl.
Row 22 Sl 1, k1, *k2, RT; rep from * to last 2 sts, end k1, k1tbl.
Row 24 Sl 1, *k2, RT; rep from * to last 3 sts, k2, k1tbl.
Row 26 Sl 1, k1, *RT, k2; rep from * to last 2 sts, k1, k1tbl.
Row 28 Sl 1, *RT, k2; rep from * to last 3 sts, k2, k1tbl.
Rows 29–36 Rep rows 21–28.
Rows 37–40 With CC, purl.
Rep rows 1–40 for zigzag pat.

WRAP
With MC, cast on 20 sts.

BEG ZIGZAG PAT
Work rows 1–40 of zigzag pat three times, then rep rows 1–36 once more. Bind off.

FINISHING
Weave in ends. Block lightly to measurements.

EDGING
With CC and crochet hook, work 1 row of sc around entire edge of wrap. Fasten off. Ch 4"/10cm length for button loop. Sl st to corner at beg of cast-on row. Sew button to opposite end of shawl. ●

2 Zigzag Capelet

KNITTED MEASUREMENTS
Length including edging 40"/101.5cm
Width including edging and buckle band
12½"/31.5cm

MATERIALS
- 2 3½oz/100g hanks (each approx 87yd/80m) of Classic Elite Yarns *Toboggan* (merino wool/superfine alpaca) in #6758 garnet (MC) (6)
- 2 hanks in #6713 ebony (CC)
- One pair size 15 (10mm) needles OR SIZE TO OBTAIN GAUGE
- One size 13 (9mm) circular needle, 24"/61cm long
- Size 8/H (5mm) crochet hook
- One 2"/5cm rhinestone buckle
- One sew-on snap

GAUGE
11 sts and 15 rows = 4"/10cm over zigzag pattern using larger needles.
TAKE TIME TO CHECK GAUGE.

STITCH GLOSSARY
LT Knit into back of second st on LH needle without dropping st from LH needle, then knit first 2 sts on LH needle together through back loops.
Drop both sts from LH needle.
RT K2tog but do not slip from needle; insert RH needle between the sts just knitted tog and knit the first stitch again, then slip both stitches from the needle together.
kfb Knit into front and back of stitch—1 st increased.
pfb Purl into front and back of stitch—1 st increased.

ZIGZAG PATTERN
(over a multiple of 4 sts)
Rows 1, 3, 5, 7, and 9 (WS) With MC, sl 1, p to last st, k1tbl.
Row 2 Sl 1, *LT, k2; rep from * to last 3 sts, LT, k1tbl.
Row 4 Sl 1, k1, *LT, k2; rep from * to last 2 sts, end k1, k1tbl.
Row 6 Sl 1, *k2, LT; rep from * to last 3 sts, k2, k1tbl.
Row 8 Sl 1, k1, *k2, LT; rep from * to last 2 sts, k1, k1tbl.
Row 10 Sl 1, *LT, k2; rep from * to last 3 sts, LT, k1tbl.
Rows 11–14 With CC, purl.
Rows 15, 17, 19, 21, and 23 (WS) With MC, sl 1, p to last st, k1tbl.
Row 16 Sl 1, *RT, k2; rep from * to last 3 sts, end k2, k1tbl.
Row 18 Sl 1, k1, *k2, RT; rep from * to last 2 sts, end k1, k1tbl.
Row 20 Sl 1, *k2, RT; rep from * to last 3 sts, k2, k1tbl.
Row 22 Sl 1, k1, *RT, k2; rep from * to last 2 sts, k1, k1tbl.

Row 24 Sl 1, *RT, k2; rep from * to last 3 sts, k2, k1tbl.
Rows 25–28 With CC, purl.
Rep rows 1–28 for zigzag pat.

CAPELET
With MC and larger needles, cast on 28 sts.

BEG ZIGZAG PAT
Work rows 1–28 of zigzag pat 4 times, then rep rows 1–10 once more. Bind off.

FINISHING
Weave in ends. Block lightly to measurements.

BUCKLE BAND
Next row (RS) With circular needle, CC, and RS of capelet facing, cast on 16 sts to LH needle, knit these sts, place marker, then pick up and knit 120 sts across right side edge (beg of RS rows) of capelet—136 sts. Do not join.
Next (dec) row (WS) K2, [k2tog, k3] to 3 sts before marker, k2tog, k1, sl marker, k16—112 sts.
Knit [2 rows MC, 2 rows CC] twice.
Work in St st and CC for 2"/5cm. Bind off. Fold St st to WS of band and sew in place along pickup row.

EDGING
With CC and crochet hook, work 1 row sc around 3 rem edges of capelet.
Fasten off. Overlap band with loose strap on top. Sew buckle to band above final 4-row stripe of CC. Sew one half of snap to RS of inside corner of band, the other half to WS of band to support buckle. ●

③ Zigzag Cowl

KNITTED MEASUREMENTS
Length including edging 45"/114cm
Width including edging 7½"/19cm

MATERIALS
- 2 3½oz/100g hanks (each approx 87yd/80m) of Classic Elite Yarns *Toboggan* (merino wool/superfine alpaca) in #6731 periwinkle (MC) 🔵
- 1 hank in #6713 ebony (CC)
- One pair each sizes 13 (9mm) and 15 (10mm) needles OR SIZE TO OBTAIN GAUGE
- Size 8/H (5mm) crochet hook
- 3 1¼"/3cm buttons

GAUGE
11 sts and 15 rows = 4"/10cm over zigzag pattern, using larger needles.
TAKE TIME TO CHECK GAUGE.

STITCH GLOSSARY
LT Knit into back of second st on LH needle without dropping st from LH needle, then knit first 2 sts on LH needle together through back loops. Drop both sts from LH needle.
RT K2tog but do not slip from needle. Insert RH needle between the sts just knitted tog and knit the first stitch again, then slip both stitches from the needle together.

ZIGZAG PATTERN
(over a multiple of 4 sts)
Rows 1, 3, 5, and 7 (WS) With MC, sl 1, p to last st, k1tbl.
Row 2 Sl 1, *LT, k2; rep from * to last 3 sts, LT, k1tbl.
Row 4 Sl 1, k1, *LT, k2; rep from * to last 2 sts, end k1, k1tbl.
Row 6 S1, *k2, LT; rep from * to last 3 sts, k2, k1tbl.
Row 8 Sl 1, k1, *k2, LT; rep from * to last 2 sts, k1, k1tbl.
Rows 9–16 Rep rows 1–8.
Rows 17–20 With MC, purl.
Rows 21, 23, 25, and 27 (WS) Sl 1, p to last st, k1tbl.
Row 22 Sl 1, k1, *k2, RT; rep from * to last 2 sts, end k1, k1tbl.
Row 24 Sl 1, *k2, RT; rep from * to last 3 sts, k2, k1tbl.
Row 26 Sl 1, k1, *RT, k2; rep from * to last 2 sts, k1, k1tbl.
Row 28 Sl 1, *RT, k2; rep from * to last 3 sts, k2, k1tbl.
Rows 29–36 Rep rows 21–28.
Rows 37–40 With MC, purl.
Rep rows 1–40 for zigzag pattern.

COWL
BUTTONHOLE BAND
With smaller needles and CC, cast on 20 sts. Purl 3 rows.
Next (buttonhole) row (WS) P2, bind off 3 sts, p until there are 4 sts on RH needle, bind off 3 sts, p until there are 3 sts on RH needle, bind off 3 sts, p to end.
Next row P across, casting on 3 sts over each buttonhole. Purl 3 more rows.

BEG ZIGZAG PAT
Change to larger needles and MC.
Work rows 1–40 of zigzag pat 3 times, then rep rows 1–36 once more.

BUTTON BAND
Change to smaller needles and CC.
Purl 8 rows. Bind off.

FINISHING
Weave in ends. Block lightly to measurements.

EDGING
With CC and crochet hook, work 1 row of sc along both long side edges from cast-on row to bind-off row. Sew buttons to button band opposite buttonholes. ●

•Rich Ruffles

TONIA BARRY turns up the heat, creating three spectacular cover-ups in warm shades of rust, orange, and red. Ruffled edges frame the allover lace-and-bobbles stitch patterns.

1 The RUFFLED COWL features a dramatic asymmetrical shape. Knit in merino and silk *Magnolia*, it is a neck warmer fit for a queen.

2 A lightweight RUFFLED SCARF worked in *Silky Alpaca Lace* shows a delicate version of the lace, bobbles, and ruffles motif.

3 This RUFFLED WRAP is bright, lively, and as fun as it is functional. *Firefly* shows off its magnificent sheen and drape here in a warm shade of orange.

1 Ruffled Cowl

KNITTED MEASUREMENTS
Circumference 23"/58.5cm
Length 11"/28cm (blocked)

MATERIALS
- 3 1¾oz/50g balls (each approx 120yd/109m) of Classic Elite Yarns *Magnolia* (merino/silk) in #5478 terra cotta (**3**)
- One size 6 (4mm) circular needle, 24"/61cm long, OR SIZE TO OBTAIN GAUGE
- Cable needle (cn)
- Stitch markers

GAUGE
22 sts and 27 rnds = 4"/10cm over lace & bobbles chart (blocked). TAKE TIME TO CHECK GAUGE.

STITCH GLOSSARY
Bobble (K1, yo) twice, k1, turn, p5, turn, slip 2 sts, k3, pass the 2 slipped sts over the k3.
Kf&b Knit into the front and back of st.
4-st LC Sl 1 st to cn and hold in front, k3, k1 from cn.
4-st RC Sl 3 sts to cn and hold in back, k1, k3 from cn.
W&T (wrap and turn) (RS) Wyib, sl next st purlwise onto RH needle, bring yarn to front of work, return slipped st to LH needle, bring yarn to back of work, turn.
W&T (wrap and turn) (WS) Wyif, sl next st purlwise onto RH needle, bring yarn to back of work, return slipped st to LH needle, bring yarn to front of work, turn.
Hide wrap (RS) Pick up the wrap from the front with the RH needle and knit together with the st it wraps.
Hide wrap (WS) Pick up the wrap from the back with the RH needle and purl together with the st it wraps.

COWL
Cast on 128 sts. Place marker (pm) for beg of rnd and join, being careful not to twist sts.

BEG CHART PAT
Work 16-st rep 8 times, then repeat rnds 1–12 five times.
Next (inc) row [Kf&b] 64 times. Bind off rem 64 sts—128 sts.
Ruffle Knit 128 sts. Place a marker on cast-on edge 5"/13cm to the left of last st worked, pm; then, working on the diagonal, pick up and knit 1 st in each row down to the cast-on row marker (60 sts), pm; with WS facing, pick up and purl 35 sts along cast-on edge to cast-on tail—223 sts. Turn work.
Row 1 (WS) Working back and forth, [kf&b] 35 times, purl rem sts—258 sts.

Row 2 Knit to marker, [kf&b] 60 times to next marker, purl to last 8 sts, w&t—318 sts.
Row 3 Knit to marker, purl to last 8 sts, w&t.
Row 4 Knit to marker, purl until 8 sts rem before previous wrap, w&t. Rep last row 9 times more.
Next row Knit to marker, purl to the end, hiding wraps as you come to them. Bind off all sts, hiding wraps as you come to them.

FINISHING
Weave in ends. Lightly block to measurements. ●

LACE & BOBBLES CHART (RNDS)

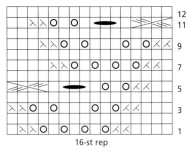

16-st rep

Stitch Key

☐ Knit   ⊠ Ssk
Ⓞ Yo   4-st RC
━ Bobble   4-st LC
⊠ K2tog

2 Ruffled Scarf

KNITTED MEASUREMENTS
Width 14"/35.5cm
Length 68"/172.5cm (blocked)

MATERIALS
- 3 1¾oz/50g balls (each approx 440yd/402m) of Classic Elite Yarns *Silky Alpaca Lace* (alpaca/silk) in #2453 berry (1)
- One pair size 4 (3.5mm) kneedles OR SIZE TO OBTAIN GAUGE
- Cable needle (cn)
- Stitch markers

GAUGE
26 sts and 29 rows = 4"/10cm over lace & bobbles chart (blocked).
TAKE TIME TO CHECK GAUGE.

STITCH GLOSSARY
See page 82.

RIGHT-SIDE SHORT ROWS
Row 1 (RS) K10, w&t.
Row 2 P10.
Row 3 K8, w&t.
Row 4 P8.
Row 5 K6, w&t.
Row 6 P6.
Row 7 K4, w&t.
Row 8 P4.

LEFT-SIDE SHORT ROWS
Row 1 (WS) P10, w&t.
Row 2 K10.
Row 3 P8, w&t.
Row 4 K8.
Row 5 P6, w&t.
Row 6 K6.
Row 7 P4, w&t.
Row 8 K4.

SCARF
Loosely cast on 152 sts. Purl 1 row.
*Work right side short rows.
Next row (RS) Knit across, hiding all wraps.
Next row (WS) Work left side short rows.
Next row (WS) Purl across, hiding all wraps. Work 6 rows in St st. Rep from * twice more.
Next row (RS) Work right side short rows.
Next row (RS) K12, hiding wraps, [k2tog] 64 times, k12—88 sts.
Next row (WS) Work left side short rows.
Next row (WS) Purl across, hiding all wraps.

BEG CHART PAT
Row 1 (RS) Work 12 sts in St st, place marker (pm), rep 16 sts of lace & bobbles chart 4 times, pm, work rem 12 sts in St st. Work 5 rows even in pats as est.
**Next row (RS) Work right side short rows.
Next row (RS) K12, hiding wraps, cont in lace & bobbles chart as est, repeating rows 1–12; k12.
Next row (WS) Work left side short rows.

Next row (WS) P12, hiding all wraps, cont in lace & bobbles chart as est, p12. Work even in pats as est for 6 rows.
Rep from ** until 38 reps of chart have been worked.
Next (inc) row (RS) K12, [kf&b] 64 times, k12—152 sts. Purl 1 row.
Next row (RS) *Work right side short rows.
Next row (RS) Knit across, hiding all wraps.
Next row (WS) Work left side short rows.
Next row (WS) Purl across, hiding all wraps. Work 6 rows in St st. Rep from * twice more.
Bind off all sts as follows: K1, *k1, return the 2 sts back to LH needle, k2tog tbl; rep from * across.

FINISHING
Weave in ends. Lightly block to measurements. ●

LACE & BOBBLES CHART (ROWS)

16-st rep

Stitch Key
- ☐ K on RS, p on WS
- �O Yo
- ⬤ Bobble
- ◢ K2tog
- ◣ Ssk
- 4-st RC
- 4-st LC

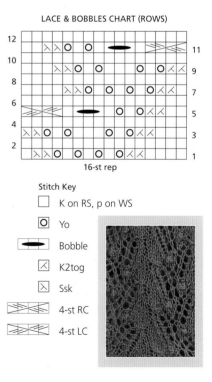

RIGHT-SIDE SHORT ROWS

Row 1 (RS) K10, w&t.
Row 2 P10.
Row 3 K8, w&t.
Row 4 P8.
Row 5 K6, w&t.
Row 6 P6.
Row 7 K4, w&t.
Row 8 P4.

LEFT-SIDE SHORT ROWS

Row 1 (WS) P10, w&t.
Row 2 K10.
Row 3 P8, w&t.
Row 4 K8.
Row 5 P6, w&t.
Row 6 K6.
Row 7 P4, w&t.
Row 8 K4.

WRAP

Loosely cast on 188 sts. Purl 1 row.
*Work right side short rows.
Next row (RS) Knit across, hiding all wraps.
Next row (WS) Work left side short rows.
Next row (WS) Purl across, hiding all wraps. Work 6 rows in St st. Rep from * twice more.
Next row (RS) Work right side short rows.
Next row (RS) K14, hiding wraps, [k2tog] 80 times, k14—108 sts.
Next row (WS) Work left side short rows.
Next row (WS) Purl across, hiding all wraps.

BEG CHART PAT

Row 1 (RS) Work 14 sts in St st, place marker (pm), rep 16 sts of lace & bobbles chart 5 times, pm, work rem 14 sts in St st. Work 5 rows even in pats as est.
**Next row (RS) Work right side short rows.
Next row (RS) K14, hiding wraps, cont in lace & bobbles chart as est, repeating rows 1–12; k14.

Next row (WS) Work left side short rows.
Next row (WS) P14, hiding all wraps, cont in lace & bobbles chart as est, p14. Work even in pats as est for 6 rows.
Rep from ** until piece measures 70"/177.5cm from beg, ending with a WS row.
Next (inc) row (RS) K14, [kf&b] 80 times, k14—188 sts. Purl 1 row.
Next row (RS) *Work right side short rows.
Next row (RS) Knit across, hiding all wraps.
Next row (WS) Work left side short rows.
Next row (WS) Purl across, hiding all wraps. Work 6 rows in St st. Rep from * twice more.
Bind off all sts as follows: K1, *k1, return the 2 sts back to LH needle, k2tog tbl; rep from * across.

FINISHING

Weave in ends. Lightly block to measurements. ●

---

3 Ruffled Wrap

KNITTED MEASUREMENTS
Width 18"/45.5cm
Length 74"/188cm

MATERIALS
- 9 1¾oz/50g balls (each approx 155yd/142m) of Classic Elite Yarns *Firefly* (viscose/linen) in #7755 corsica **2**
- One pair size size 5 (3.75mm) needles OR SIZE TO OBTAIN GAUGE
- Cable needle (cn)
- Stitch markers

GAUGE
24 sts and 28 rows = 4"/10cm over lace & bobbles chart (blocked).
TAKE TIME TO CHECK GAUGE.

STITCH GLOSSARY
See page 82.

LACE & BOBBLES CHART (ROWS)

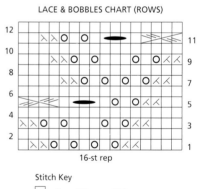

16-st rep

Stitch Key

☐	K on RS, p on WS
Ⓞ	Yo
▬	Bobble
⟋	K2tog
⟍	Ssk
⟩⟨	4-st RC
⟩⟨	4-st LC

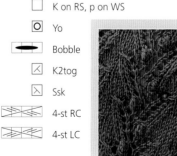

• Light & Lacy

JACQUELINE VAN DILLEN's trio of lace wraps brings to mind shades of blue and green sea glass. Any one would make a perfect cover-up for strolling along the ocean.

1 This CHUNKY LACE STOLE is worked in unbelievably soft merino *Ariosa*. The allover lace pattern keeps it from being too heavy.

2 This luscious design is simply a rectangle that has been partially seamed to create a sumptuous HOODED SCARF.

3 This LIGHT LACE WRAP is knit in two halves and seamed. A pretty leaf lace border follows the curve.

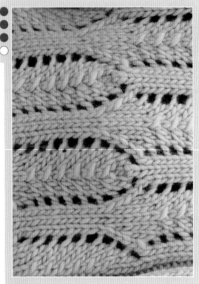

KNITTED MEASUREMENTS
Length approx 17 x 56"/43 x 142cm

MATERIALS
- 6 1¾oz/50g balls (each approx 87yd/80m) of Classic Elite Yarns *Ariosa* (extrafine merino) in #4846 bermuda (5)
- One pair size 7 (4.5mm) needles OR SIZE TO OBTAIN GAUGE

GAUGE
14 sts and 16 rows = 4"/10 cm over chart pat using size 7 (4.5mm) needles. TAKE TIME TO CHECK GAUGE.

STOLE
Cast on 55 sts.
Row 1 (WS) Knit.
Next row K1, *yo, k2tog; rep from *, end yo, k1—56 sts.
Knit 1 row, purl 1 row, knit 1 row.

BEG CHART
Next row (RS) Work row 1 of chart to rep line, work 10 st rep twice, work to end of chart.
Cont to work chart in this manner through row 36. Rep rows 1–36 until piece measures approx 55"/139.5cm from beg, end with a row 35.
Next row (WS) Work row 36 over leaf pat 1, k21, work row 36 over leaf pat 2. Purl 1 row. Knit 1 row, dec 1 st halfway across.
Next row (RS) K1, *yo, k2tog; rep from *, end yo, k1. Bind off knitwise. ●

Stitch Key
- □ K on RS, p on WS
- — P on RS, k on WS
- O Yo
- ╱ K2tog
- ╲ Ssk
- ⅄ SK2P

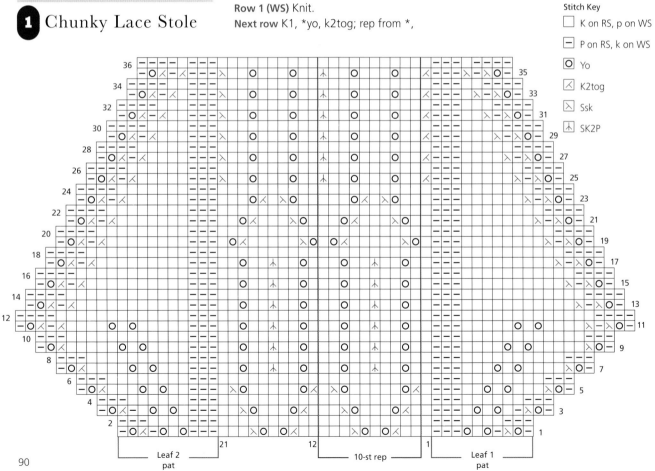

1 Chunky Lace Stole

2 Hooded Scarf

KNITTED MEASUREMENTS
Length approx 43"/109cm
Width approx 18"/45.5cm

MATERIALS
- 4 1¾oz/50g balls (each approx 230yd/210m) of Classic Elite Yarns *Giselle* (kid mohair/wool/nylon) in #4104 myrtle (3)
- One pair size 7 (4.5mm) needles OR SIZE TO OBTAIN GAUGE

GAUGE
12 sts and 16 rows = 4"/10 cm over chart pat using size 7 (4.5mm) needles. TAKE TIME TO CHECK GAUGE.

SCARF
Cast on 70 sts.

BEG CHART
Row 1 (RS) Work to rep line, work 10-st rep 5 times, work to st 21, k1.
Next row (WS) K1, beg with st 21 work to rep line, work 10-st rep 5 times, work to end of chart.
Cont to work chart in this manner through row 36. Rep rows 1–36 until piece measures 86"/218cm from beg. Bind off.

FINISHING
Weave in ends. Block to measurements. Fold in half lengthwise and sew 12"/30.5cm seam down from fold along straight edge. ●

Stitch Key
- ☐ K on RS, p on WS
- ⊟ P on RS, k on WS
- ◯ Yo
- ⟋ K2tog
- ⟍ Ssk
- ⋏ SK2P

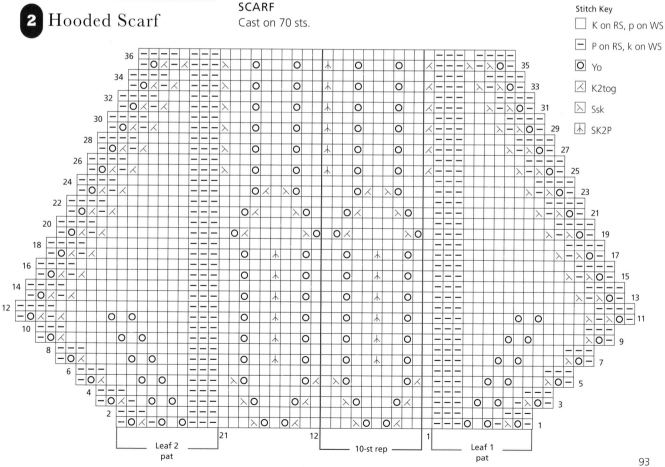

Light Lace Wrap

KNITTED MEASUREMENTS
Width 46"/162.5cm
Length 23"/58.5cm

MATERIALS
- 6 1¾oz/50g balls (each approx 128yd/117m) of Classic Elite Yarns *Kumara* (extrafine merino/baby camel) in #5792 royce mountain (4)
- One pair size 9 (5.5mm) needles OR SIZE TO OBTAIN GAUGE
- Stitch marker
- Stitch holders

GAUGE
20 sts and 24 rows = 4"/10cm over chart pattern using size 9 (5.5mm) needles.
TAKE TIME TO CHECK GAUGE.

RIGHT HALF
Cast on 142 sts and knit 3 rows.

BEG CHART
Row 1 (RS) Work 10 sts of leaf 1 pat, pm, work to rep line, work 10-st rep 12 times, work sts 12–21, k3.
Next row (WS) P3, work row 2 to rep line, work 10-st rep 12 times, sl marker, work row 2 of leaf 1 pat to end of chart.
Next (dec) row (RS) Work to marker, sl marker, k2tog, work in pat as established to end.
Cont to foll chart in this manner and rep dec row every RS row until row 36 is complete. Rep rows 1–36 twice more, cont to dec every RS row.
Place 8 leaf pat sts on a st holder—81 sts.

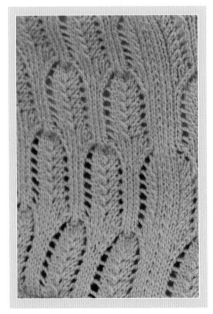

Rep rows 1–17 once more, binding off 6 sts at beg of each RS row.
Work one row even. Bind off rem 27 sts.

LEFT HALF
Cast on 141 sts and knit 3 rows.

BEG CHART
Row 1 (RS) K3, work from st 1 to rep line, work 10-st rep 12 times, work to st 21, pm, work to end of chart, working leaf pat 2.
Next (dec) row (WS) Work to marker, sl marker, p2tog, foll chart pat as established to end of row.
Complete to correspond to right half by working decs and binding off on WS rows.

COMPLETE EDGING
Place leaf pat 1 sts on needle and rep rows 1–36 three times more. Bind off.
Rep for leaf pat 2 sts.

FINISHING
Sew the 2 halves of shawl tog along
the straight center side. Sew the leaf lace edgings to the edges of the shawl. ●

③ Light Lace Wrap

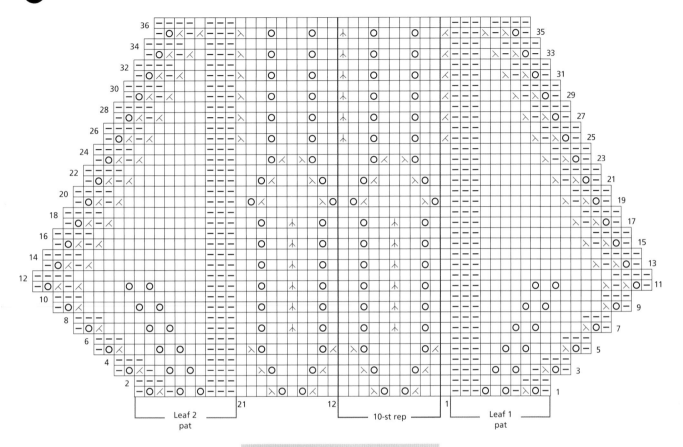

Stitch Key

- ☐ K on RS, p on WS
- — P on RS, k on WS
- ⊙ Yo
- ╱ K2tog
- ╲ Ssk
- ⋏ SK2P

• Linen Stitch

JILL GUTMAN SCHOENFUSS takes one stitch–half linen–and works it three ways to create three very different scarves.

1 This VARIEGATED SCARF uses half linen stitch and ribbing to create complex textures and color changes courtesy of multicolored *Liberty Wool Light.*

2 Knit in a basic half linen stitch, this THREE-COLOR SCARF gives the impression of a complex Fair Isle pattern, while in fact only one color is worked at a time.

3 A SOLID-COLOR SCARF is worked between half linen stitch and half linen rib. A flirty ruffle on either end adds a touch of charm.

from * across, ending k1.
Rows 2 and 4 *P3, k3; rep from * to end, ending p3.
Row 3 K2, sl 1 wyif, *p3, sl 1 wyif, k1, sl 1 wyif; rep from * to last 6 sts, p3, sl 1 wyif, k2.
Rep rows 1–4 for half linen rib.

SCARF

With size 4 (3.5mm) needles, cast on 33 sts. Work in half linen rib until piece measures 4"/10cm, ending with row 4. Change to size 6 (4mm) needles. Work in half linen rib as follows:
Row 1 (RS) K1, sl 1 wyif, k1, p3, [k1, sl 1 wyif] 10 times, k1, p3, k1, sl 1 wyif, k1.
Rows 2 and 4 P3, k3, p21, k3, p3.
Row 3 K2, sl 1 wyif, p3, [sl 1 wyif, k1] 10 times, sl 1 wyif, p3, sl 1 wyif, k2.
Rep rows 1–4 until piece measures 56"/142cm, ending with row 4. Change to size 4 (3.5mm) needles. Work in half linen rib until piece measures 60"/152cm. Bind off in pat.

FINISHING

Weave in ends. Block to measurements. ●

1 Variegated Scarf

KNITTED MEASUREMENTS
Width 4"/10cm (after blocking)
Length 66"/167cm (after blocking)

MATERIALS
● 2 1¾oz/50g balls (each approx 200yd/182m) of Classic Elite Yarns *Liberty Wool Light* (washable wool) in #6691 north sea whitecaps (**2**)
● One pair each size 6 (4mm) and size 4 (3.5mm) needles OR SIZE TO OBTAIN GAUGE

GAUGES
24 sts and 32 rows = 4"/10cm over St st using size 6 (4mm) needles.

28 sts and 40 rows = 4"/10cm over half linen st using size 6 (4mm) needles.
TAKE TIME TO CHECK GAUGES.

HALF LINEN RIB
(over a multiple of 6 sts plus 3)
Row 1 (RS) *K1, sl 1 wyif, k1, p3; rep

HALF LINEN STITCH

(over a multiple of 2 sts plus 1)
Row 1 (RS) K1, *sl 1 wyif, k1;
rep from * to end.
Rows 2 and 4 Purl.
Row 3 K2, *sl 1 wyif, k1;
rep from * to last st, k1.
Rep rows 1–4 for half linen st.

SCARF

With MC, cast on 25 sts. Knit 1 row,
purl 1 row. Change to half linen stitch.
*With CC1, work in pat for 2 rows.
With CC2, work in pat for 2 rows. With
MC, work in pat for 2 rows.
Rep from * until piece measures
60"/152cm, ending with MC on a WS
row. Knit 1 row. Bind off.

FINISHING

Weave in ends. Block to measurements.

FRINGE

Cut 8"/20.5cm lengths of all
colors. Holding in groups of 2 strands,
join fringe to ends of scarf with
crochet hook. ●

2 Three-Color Scarf

KNITTED MEASUREMENTS
Width 5½"/14cm
Length 60"/152cm

MATERIALS
● 1 1¾oz/50g balls (each approx
  87yd/80m) of Classic Elite Yarns *Ariosa*
  (extrafine merino)
  each in #4814 slate gray (MC),
  #4813 basalt (CC1), and
  #4801 cloud (CC2) (⑤)
● One pair size 10½ (6.5mm) needles

OR SIZE TO OBTAIN GAUGE
● Size K/10½ (6.5mm) crochet hook
  (for fringe)

GAUGES
14 sts and 20 rows = 4"/10 cm over St
st using size 10½ (6.5mm) needles.

18 sts and 20 rows = 4"/10 cm
over half linen st using size 10½
(6.5mm) needles.
TAKE TIME TO CHECK GAUGES.

26 sts and 36 rows = 4"/10 cm over half linen st using size 6 (4mm) needles.
TAKE TIME TO CHECK GAUGES.

HALF LINEN STITCH
(over a multiple of 2 sts plus 1)
Row 1 (RS) K1, *sl 1 wyif, k1; rep from * to end.
Rows 2 and 4 Purl.
Row 3 K2, *sl 1 wyif, k1; rep from * to last st, k1.
Rep rows 1–4 for half linen st.

HALF LINEN RIB
(over a multiple of 6 sts plus 3)
Row 1 (RS) *K1, sl 1 wyif, k1, p3; rep from * across, ending k1.
Rows 2 and 4 *P3, k3; rep from * to end, ending p3.
Row 3 K2, sl 1 wyif, *p3, sl 1 wyif, k1, sl 1 wyif; rep from * to last 6 sts, p3, sl 1 wyif, k2.
Rep rows 1–4 for half linen rib.

SCARF
With size 6 (4mm) needles, cast on 78 sts. Work in garter st (knit every row) for 8 rows.
Next row (RS) *K2tog; rep from * across—39 sts. Purl 1 row.
Work in half linen stitch until piece measures 4"/10cm, ending with row 4. Change to size 4 (3.5mm) Work in half linen rib until piece measures 48"/121.5cm, ending with a WS row. Change to size 6 (4mm) needles. Work in half linen stitch until piece measures 51"/129.5cm, ending with a WS row.
Next row (RS) *Kfb; rep from * across—78 sts.
Work in garter st for 8 rows. Bind off.

FINISHING
Weave in ends. Block to measurements. ●

3 Solid-Color Scarf

KNITTED MEASUREMENTS
Width at ribbing 4½"/11cm
Length 52"/132cm

MATERIALS
● 3 1¾oz/50g balls (each approx 118yd/107m) of Classic Elite Yarns *Wool Bam Boo* (wool/bamboo) in #1692 true blue (3)
● One pair each size 6 (4mm) and size 4 (3.5mm) needles OR SIZE TO OBTAIN GAUGE

GAUGES
22 sts and 28 rows = 4"/10cm over St st using size 6 (4mm) needles.

• Fun & Funky

IRINA POLUDNENKO's whimsical scarves are wearable art. All three take basic embellishments—bobbles, I-cords, loops—and showcase them to create stunning results.

1 I-cords are not just for embellishments! For this I-CORD SCARF, long strands are anchored at either end with striped garter-ridge knitting.

2 This vibrant ZIGZAG SCARF makes good use of short rows to create a dynamic pattern punctuated with perky bobbles.

3 The garter stitch loops of this clever LOOP SCARF are knit and joined together as you go. The ribbed trim is then picked up and knit along the edge.

1 I-Cord Scarf

KNITTED MEASUREMENTS
Width approx 6"/15cm
Length approx 62"/157.5cm

MATERIALS
- 2 1¾oz/50g balls (each approx 103yd/94m) of Classic Elite Yarns *Chesapeake* (organic cotton/merino wool) each in #5955 shanghai red (A) and #5985 mandarin orange (B) (4)
- 1 ball each in #5932 berry (C) and #5906 tigerlily (D)
- One pair size 7 (4.5mm) double-pointed needles (dpns) OR SIZE TO OBTAIN GAUGE
- Stitch holders

GAUGE
20 sts and 32 rows to 4"/10cm over stockinette stitch using size 7 (4.5mm) dpns.
TAKE TIME TO CHECK GAUGE.

NOTE
Slip first st and purl last st every row.

SCARF
With A, cast on 30 sts. Purl 1 row, knit 1 row. Cut A. *Join B, knit 1 row, purl 1 row, knit 1 row. Cut B. Join C, knit 1 row, purl 1 row, knit 1 row. Cut C. Join D, knit 1 row, purl 1 row, knit 1 row. Cut D. Join A, knit 1 row, purl 1 row, knit 1 row. Cut A. Rep from * 13 times more.

I-CORDS
With A, k3, M1—4 sts.
**Work in I-cord for 49"/124.5cm. Cut yarn and leave sts on holder.
*** With B, M1, k2, M1—4 sts. Rep from ** to *** to form next I-cord. Cont making cords as for last, following color sequence [C, D, A, B], until 3 sts rem.
Last cord M1, k3—4 sts.
Rep from ** to ***.

JOIN I-CORDS
Next row With B k2, k2tog across first cord, ****(k2tog) twice; rep from **** to last cord, k2tog, k2—30 sts.
Resume stripe pat, rep from * 4 times more.
Last stripe Knit 1 row, purl 1 row. Bind off.

FINISHING
Weave in ends.
Block to measurements. ●

2 Zigzag Scarf

KNITTED MEASUREMENTS
Width approx 8"/20.5cm
Length approx 78"/198cm

MATERIALS
- 4 1¾oz/50g balls (each approx 103yd/94m) of Classic Elite Yarns *Chesapeake* (organic cotton/merino wool) in #5985 mandarin orange (A) (4)
- 1 ball in #5955 shanghai red (B)
- One pair size 7 (4.5mm) needles

GAUGE
20 sts and 32 rows = 4"/10cm over St stitch using size 7 (4.5mm) needle.

STITCH GLOSSARY
MB (make bobble) With B, (k1, yo, k1, yo, k1) in next st, turn, p5, turn, k5, turn, p5, turn, k1, k3tog, k1, turn, p3tog, turn, slip completed bobble from LH needle to RH needle.

SCARF
With A, cast on 27 sts. Knit 1 row.
Work in short rows as follows: *K25, wrap and turn (W&T, see page 82), knit to end. K23, W&T, knit to end. K4, M1, k17, W&T, knit to end. K20, W&T, knit to end. K18, W&T, knit to end. K4, M1, k12, W&T, knit to end. K15, W&T, knit to end. K13, W&T, knit to end. K4, M1, k7, W&T, knit to end. K10, W&T, knit to end. K8, W&T, knit to end. K4, M1, k2, W&T, knit to end. Bind off 4 sts, knit to end, knitting wraps together with st—27 sts. Knit 1 row.
Next row K2, MB, **with A, knit to end. Rep from * to **. **Next row** Knit to last 3 sts, MB, with A, k2. Knit one row***. Rep from * to *** 16 times more, omitting bobbles on last rep. Bind off.

FINISHING
Weave in ends. Block to measurements. ●

SCARF

Cast on 15 sts. Knit 10 rows.
*Next row K10, turn. Work in garter st (k every row) for 19 rows more, over these 10 sts only.
Next row Fold strip just knit, knit each of these 10 sts tog with corresponding st 20 rows below (loop formed). K5.**
Work in garter st for 15 rows.
Rep from * 27 times more. Rep from * to ** once more.
Work in garter st for 10 rows. Bind off; do not cut yarn.

TRIM

With RS facing, pick up and knit 350 sts along side edge. Work in k2, p2 rib, ending with k2, for 9 rows. Bind off in pat.

FINISHING

Weave in ends.
Block to measurements. ●

③ Loop Scarf

KNITTED MEASUREMENTS
Width approx 4½"/11.5cm
Length approx 74"/188cm

MATERIALS
● 4 1¾oz/50g balls (each approx 103yd/94m) of Classic Elite Yarns *Chesapeake* (organic cotton/merino wool) in color #5955 shanghai red ④
● One pair size 7 (4.5mm) needles OR SIZE TO OBTAIN GAUGE

GAUGE
20 sts and 32 rows = 4"/10cm over St st using size 7 (4.5mm) needles. TAKE TIME TO CHECK GAUGE.

•Short Rows

Short rows are long on style in ANGELA TONG's three dazzling designs. Featuring eyelet stitches and knit in fresh shades of yellow and green, they'll inject new life into your spring wardrobe.

1 Knit in two pieces, with the short-row section worked separately, this little leaf-colored EYELET SCARF makes a perfect first short-row project.

2 This WEDGE SCARF is worked in variegated yarn in colors reminiscent of a spring thunderstorm. Short-row shaping creates the wavy pattern.

3 Stitched in sunflower yellow, this LIGHT LACE SHAWL is the perfect light cover-up for summer.

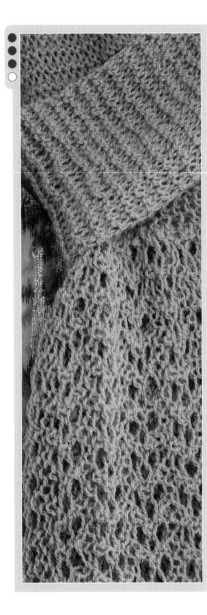

1 Eyelet Scarf

KNITTED MEASUREMENTS

Length 60"/152.5cm
Width (at neck) 2½"/6.5cm
Width (at bottom) 7½"/19cm
(after blocking)

MATERIALS

- 1 1¾oz/50g ball (each approx 440yds/402m) of Classic Elite Yarns *Silky Alpaca Lace* (alpaca/silk) in #2481 misty meadow (1)
- One pair size 6 (4.0mm) needles OR SIZE TO OBTAIN GAUGE
- Stitch holder
- Tapestry needle
- Blocking pins

GAUGE

30 sts and 36 rows = 4"/10cm
in garter st (after blocking).
TAKE TIME TO CHECK GAUGE.

SHORT ROWS

Note After each short row is completed (W&T), hide wrapped sts as instructed in following row.

W&T (Wrap & Turn)
Knit the number of stitches indicated, slip next stitch purlwise, bring yarn to front of work, return slipped stitch back to left needle, turn work, continue row as instructed—one stitch wrapped.
hide wrapped st Knit to wrapped stitch; with tip of right needle, pick up wrap and the stitch it wraps and knit tog.

FIRST SIDE

LOWER EDGE
Cast on 48 sts.
Row 1 (RS) Knit.
Row 2 Knit.
Row 3 K44, W&T, k1, *yo, k2tog; rep from * to last st, k1.
Row 4 Knit.
Row 5 K2, *k2tog, yo; rep from * to last 2 sts, k2.
Row 6 K44, W&T, k1,*yo, k2tog; rep from * to last st, k1.
Rows 7 and 8 Knit.
Row 9 K44, W&T, k44.
Row 10 K44, W&T, k1, *yo, k2tog; rep from * to last st, k1.
Row 11 Knit.
Row 12 K2, *k2tog, yo; rep from * to last 2 sts, k2.
Row 13 K44, W&T, k1, *yo, k2tog; rep from * to last st, k1.
Rows 14 and 15 Knit.
Rep rows 9–15 seven times more.
Bind off all sts. Fasten off, leaving 6"/15cm tail.

NECK
With RS facing, turn edge 90 degrees to right with short side edge facing up. Pick up and k 21 sts across.
Work garter st (knit every row) for 23"/58.5cm. Place stitches on stitch holder.

SECOND SIDE

Rep as for first side, leaving stitches on needle.

FINISHING

Transfer stitches from holder onto needle. Graft stitches tog with stitches from second needle. Weave in ends. Wet block to measurements. ●

2 Wedge Scarf

KNITTED MEASUREMENTS
Length 68"/172.5cm
Width 7"/18cm

MATERIALS
- 3 1¾oz/50g balls (each approx 122yds/112m) of Classic Elite Yarns *Liberty Wool Print* (washable wool) in #7869 leaf and bumblebee (**4**)
- One pair size 8 (5mm) needles OR SIZE TO OBTAIN GAUGE
- Tapestry needle
- Blocking pins

GAUGE
Note Make gauge swatch from Lace Pattern Section II.
14 sts and 23 rows = 4"/10cm over lace stitch pat using size 8 (5mm) needles (after blocking).
TAKE TIME TO CHECK GAUGE.

SHORT ROWS
Note After each short row is completed (W&T), hide wrapped sts as instructed in following row.

W&T (Wrap & Turn) Knit the number of stitches indicated, slip next stitch purlwise, bring yarn to front of work, return slipped stitch back to left needle, turn work, continue row as instructed—one stitch wrapped.
hide wrapped st Knit to wrapped stitch; with tip of right needle, pick up wrap and the stitch it wraps and knit tog.

SCARF
Cast on 26 sts.

LACE PATTERN SECTION I
Rows 1 and 2 Knit.
Row 3 K24, W&T, k1, *yo, k2tog; rep from * to the last st, k1.
Row 4 Knit.
Row 5 K2, *k2tog, yo; rep from * to last 2 sts, k2.
Row 6 K24, W&T, k1,*yo, k2tog; rep from * to last st, k1.
Rows 7 and 8 Knit.
Row 9 K24, W&T, k24.
Row 10 K24, W&T, k1, *yo, k2tog; rep from * to last st, k1.
Row 11 Knit.
Row 12 K2, *k2tog, yo; rep from * to last 2 sts, k2.
Row 13 K24, W&T, k1, *yo, k2tog; rep from * to last st, k1.
Rows 14 and 15 Knit.
Rep rows 9–15 twice more.
Row 16 Knit.
Row 17 K24, W&T, k24.
Row 18 K1, [k2tog, yo] 11 times, k1, W&T, k24.
Row 19 K2, *yo, k2tog; rep from ·* to last 2 sts, k2.
Row 20 Knit.
Row 21 K1, [k2tog, yo] 11 times, k1, W&T, k24.
Row 22 Knit.
Rep rows 16–22 three times more.

LACE PATTERN SECTION II
Rows 23 and 24 Knit.
Row 25 K24, W&T, k24.
Row 26 K24, W&T, k1, *yo, k2tog; rep from * to last st, k1.
Row 27 Knit.
Row 28 K2, *k2tog, yo; rep from * to last 2 sts, k2.
Row 29 K24, W&T, k1, *yo, k2tog; rep from * to last st, k1.
Rows 30 and 31 Knit.
Rep rows 25–31 three times more.
Row 32 Knit.
Row 33 K24, W&T, k24.
Row 34 K1, [k2tog, yo] 11 times, k1, W&T, k24.
Row 35 K2, *yo, k2tog; rep from * to last 2 sts, k2.
Row 36 Knit.
Row 37 K1, [k2tog, yo] 11 times, k1, W&T, k24.
Row 38 Knit.
Rep rows 32–38 three times more.
Rep rows 23–38 four times more.
Row 39 Knit.
Bind off all sts.

FINISHING
Weave in ends.
Wet block with pins to accentuate the curves and lace pattern. ●

 Light Lace Shawl

KNITTED MEASUREMENTS
Width (end to end) 71"/180cm
Length (at center point) 11"/28cm
(after blocking)

MATERIALS
- 2 1¾oz/50g balls (each approx 155yds/142m) of Classic Elite Yarns *Firefly* (viscose/linen) in #7750 leopard's bane (❷)
- One pair size 7 (4.5 mm) needles OR SIZE TO OBTAIN GAUGE
- Waste yarn (for provisional cast-on)
- Tapestry needle
- Blocking pins

GAUGE
19 sts and 30 rows = 4"/10cm in garter st using size 7 (4.5mm) needles (after blocking).
TAKE TIME TO CHECK GAUGE.

SHORT ROWS
Note After each short row is completed (W&T), hide wrapped sts as instructed in following row.
W&T (Wrap & Turn)
Knit the number of stitches indicated, slip next stitch purlwise, bring yarn to front of work, return slipped stitch back to left needle, turn work, continue row as instructed—one stitch wrapped.
hide wrapped st
Knit to wrapped stitch; with tip of right needle, pick up wrap and the stitch it wraps and knit tog.

SHAWL
CENTER PANEL (LACE PAT)
Cast on 50 sts with provisional cast-on.
Row 1 (RS) Knit.
Row 2 Knit.
Row 3 K48, W&T, k1, *yo, k2tog; rep from * to last st, k1.
Row 4 Knit.
Row 5 K2, *k2tog, yo; rep from * to last 2 sts, k2.
Row 6 K48, W&T, k1,*yo, k2tog; rep from * to last st, k1.
Rows 7 and 8 Knit.
Row 9 K48, W&T, k48.
Row 10 K48, W&T, k1, *yo, k2tog; rep from * to last st, k1.
Row 11 Knit.
Row 12 K2, *k2tog, yo; rep from * to last 2 sts, k2.
Row 13 K48, W&T, k1, *yo, k2tog; rep from * to last st, k1.
Rows 14 and 15 Knit.
Rep rows 9–15 eight times more.
Do not fasten off. Turn.

RIGHT PANEL (GARTER ST)
Row 1 (RS) K1, k2tog, knit to end.
Rows 2–4 Knit.
Rep rows 1–4 45 times more—4 sts.
Bind off all sts.

LEFT PANEL (GARTER ST)
Undo provisional cast-on. Place sts back onto needle to beg work with the WS and join yarn.
Row 1 (WS) K1, k2tog, knit to end.
Rows 2–4 Knit.
Rep rows 1–4 45 times more—4 sts.
Bind off all sts.

FINISHING
Weave in ends. Wet block to measurements. ●

•Just Peachy

Wool Bam Boo in shades of peach, melon, and coral creates a juicy palette for LINDA MEDINA's trio of lace wraps. All three are worked in a beehive and faggoting lace stitch and are finished with delicate crocheted edgings.

1 Whether loosely tied or fastened with a brooch, this TRIANGLE SHAWL provides just a touch of warmth on summer evenings.

2 A simple rectangular BEEHIVE LACE SCARF is a great way to try out the stitch pattern before adding shaping.

3 This retro COLLARED CAPELET buttons in the front for a ladylike look.

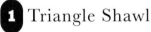

1 Triangle Shawl

KNITTED MEASUREMENTS
Width (at widest point) 19¾"/50cm
Length 51½"/130.5cm

MATERIALS
- 4 1¾oz/50g balls (each approx 118yd/108m) of Classic Elite Yarns *Wool Bam Boo* (wool/bamboo viscose) in #1612 minneola ●❸
- One pair size 7 (4.5mm) needles OR SIZE TO OBTAIN GAUGE
- One size 7 (4.5mm) circular needle, 24"/61cm long
- Size G/6 (4mm) crochet hook
- Stitch markers

GAUGE
18 sts and 27 rows = 4"/10cm over beehive and faggoting lace pattern.
TAKE TIME TO CHECK GAUGE.

BEEHIVE & FAGGOTING LACE
(over a multiple of 7 sts)
Row 1 (RS) *K2, yo, ssk, yo, SK2P, yo; rep from * to end.
Row 2 *P3, k2, yo, k2tog; rep from * to end.
Row 3 *K2, yo, ssk, k3; rep from * to end.
Row 4 Repeat row 2.
Repeat rows 1–4 for beehive & faggoting lace pat.

NOTE
When increasing and decreasing sts in lace pat, always make sure there is 1 inc paired with every dec in the pat st, not counting the inc or dec being worked. Work any odd sts appropriate to pat.

SHAWL
Using straight needles, cast on 3 sts. Beg Lace Chart and work through row 40.
Next row (RS) Cont to work in beehive & faggoting lace pat as est to last 2 sts, place marker, k2.

LACE CHART

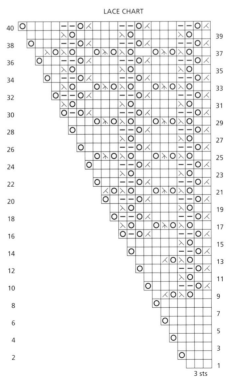

3 sts

*Next row (WS) Work highlighted section of chart row 14, then cont in pat as est to end.
Work incs into pat, using highlighted area of chart as a guide, in rows 14–40, then rep from * until you have 87 sts on needle, changing to circular needle as needed, ending with a RS row.
Next row (WS) Yo, k1, yo, k2tog, work in pat to end—88 sts.
Next row (RS) Work in pat to last 4 sts, k2, yo, ssk.
Next row P1, k1, yo, k2tog, work in pat to end.
Next row Work to last 4 sts, k2, yo, ssk.
Next (dec) row (WS) K2tog, yo, k2tog, work to end in pat—87 sts.
Cont to dec 1 st at the beg of every WS row (by k2tog), and work decs out of pattern st using the same highlighted chart section as a guide. Work until 3 sts rem. Bind off.

FINISHING
CROCHET EDGING
With RS facing and crochet hook, attach yarn to beg of bound-off edge.
Row 1 Ch1, work 140 sc evenly along the decrease edge, work 3 sc in center of point, work 140 sc evenly along increase edge, turn.
Row 2 Ch1, sl st in next 2 sts, *ch 3, sl st in last sl st, sl st in next 6 sc; rep from * to last sc, sl st in last sc. Fasten off. Lightly block to measurements. ●

Stitch Key
- ☐ K on RS, p on WS
- ⊟ P on RS, k on WS
- ⊙ Yo
- ⧄ K2tog on RS and WS
- ⧅ Ssk on RS
- ⧄ SK2P
- ☐ Highlighted area is a guide to working increased sts into pattern

2 Beehive Lace Scarf

KNITTED MEASUREMENTS
Width 7"/17.5cm
Length 55"/139.5cm

MATERIALS
- 3 1¾oz/50g balls (each approx 118yd/107m) of Classic Elite Yarns *Wool Bam Boo* (wool/bamboo viscose) in #1668 rococco orange
- One pair size 7 (4.5mm) needles OR SIZE TO OBTAIN GAUGE
- Size G/6 (4mm) crochet hook

GAUGE
18 sts and 27 rows = 4"/10cm over beehive and faggoting lace pattern. TAKE TIME TO CHECK GAUGE.

BEEHIVE & FAGGOTING LACE
(over a multiple of 7 sts plus 4)
Row 1 (RS) *K2, yo, ssk, yo, SK2P, yo; rep from * to last 4 sts, k2, yo, ssk.
Row 2 *K2, yo, k2tog, p3; rep from * to last 4 sts, k2, yo, k2tog.
Row 3 *K2, yo, ssk, k3; rep from * to last 4 sts, k2, yo, ssk.
Row 4 Repeat row 2.
Repeat rows 1–4 for beehive & faggoting lace pat.

SCARF
Cast on 32 sts. Beg beehive & faggoting lace pat and repeat rows 1–4 until piece measures approx 55"/139.5cm, ending with row 4.
Bind off.

FINISHING
CROCHET EDGING
With RS facing and crochet hook, attach yarn to beg of cast-on edge.
Row 1 Ch1, sc in each st across—32 sts.
Row 2 Ch1, sl st in next 2 sts, *ch 3, sl st in last sl st, sl st in next 6 sc; rep from * to last sc, sl st in last sc. Fasten off.
Rep edging on bound-off end of scarf.
Lightly block to measurements.●

3 Collared Capelet

KNITTED MEASUREMENTS
Circumference (buttoned) 28"/71cm
Length 14"/35.5cm

MATERIALS
- 4 1¾oz/50g balls (each approx 118yd/107m) of Classic Elite *Wool Bam Boo* (wool/bamboo viscose) in #1689 watermelon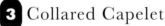
- One size 7 (4.5mm) circular needle, 36"/91cm long, OR SIZE TO OBTAIN GAUGE
- size G/6 (4mm) crochet hook
- Stitch markers
- One ¾" button

GAUGE
18 sts and 27 rows = 4"/10cm over beehive and faggoting lace pattern. TAKE TIME TO CHECK GAUGE.

BEEHIVE & FAGGOTING LACE
(over a multiple of 7 sts plus 4)
Row 1 (RS) *K2, yo, ssk, yo, SK2P, yo; rep from * to last 4 sts, k2, yo, ssk.
Row 2 *K2, yo, k2tog, p3; rep from * to last 4 sts, k2, yo, k2tog.
Rows 3 *K2, yo, ssk, k3; rep from * to last 4 sts, k2, yo, ssk.
Row 4 Repeat row 2.
Repeat rows 1–4 for beehive & faggoting lace pat.

CAPELET
Cast on 200 sts. Working back and forth on circular needles, beg beehive & faggoting lace pat and work rows 1–4 a total of 11 times.

Dec row 1 (RS) *[K2, yo, ssk, yo, SK2P, yo] twice, place marker (pm), k2tog, yo, ssk, yo, SK2P, yo, pm*; rep from * to * once, **k2, yo, ssk, yo, SK2P, yo, pm, k2tog, yo, ssk, yo, SK2P, yo, pm**; rep from ** to ** once; rep from * to * 3 times; rep from ** to ** 2 times; rep from * to * once, [k2, yo, ssk, yo, SK2P, yo] twice, k2, yo, ssk—190 sts.
Next row (WS) K2, yo, k2tog, *[p3, k2, yo, k2tog] twice, p3, k2, p1 *; rep from * to * once, **p3, k2, yo, k2tog, p3, k2, p1**; rep from ** to ** once; rep from * to * 3 times; rep from ** to ** 2 times; rep from * to * once, [p3, k2, yo, k2tog] twice.

Dec row 2 *[K2, yo, ssk, k3] twice, k2tog, yo, ssk, k2*; rep from * to * once, **k2, yo, ssk, k3, k2tog, yo, ssk, k2**; rep from ** to ** once; rep from * to * 3 times; rep from ** to ** 2 times; rep from * to * once, [k2, yo, ssk, k3] twice, k2, yo, ssk—180 sts.

Next row (WS) K2, yo, k2tog, *[p3, k2, yo, k2tog] twice, p1, k2, yo, k2tog*; rep from * to * once, **p3, k2, yo, k2tog, p1, k2, yo, k2tog**; rep from ** to ** once; rep from * to * 3 times; rep from ** to ** twice; rep from * to * once, [p3, k2, yo, k2tog] twice.

Dec row 3 *[K2, yo, ssk, yo, SK2P, yo] twice, ssk, yo, SK2P, yo*; rep from * to * once, **k2, yo, ssk, yo, SK2P, yo, ssk, yo, SK2P, yo**; rep from ** to ** once; rep from * to * 3 times; rep from ** to ** twice; rep from * to * once, [k2, yo, ssk, yo, SK2P, yo] twice, k2, yo, ssk—170 sts.

Next row (WS) K2, yo, k2tog, *[p3, k2, yo, k2tog] twice, p3, k1*; rep from * to * once, **p3, k2, yo, k2tog, p3, k1**; rep from ** to ** once; rep from * to * 3 times; rep from ** to ** twice; rep from * to * once, [p3, k2, yo, k2tog] twice.

Dec row 4 *[K2, yo, ssk, k3] twice, p2tog, p2*; rep from * to * once, **k2, yo, ssk, k3, p2tog, p2**; rep from ** to ** once; rep from * to * 3 times; rep from ** to ** twice; rep from * to * once, [k2, yo, ssk, k3] twice, k2, yo, ssk—160 sts.

Next row (WS) K2, yo, k2tog, *[p3, k2, yo, k2tog] twice, p3*; rep from * to * once, **p3, k2, yo, k2tog, p3**; rep from ** to ** once; rep from * to * 3 times; rep from ** to ** twice; rep from * to * once, [p3, k2, yo, k2tog] twice.

Dec row 5 *[K2, yo, ssk, yo, SK2P, yo] twice, k1, k2tog*; rep from * to * once, **k2, yo, ssk, yo, SK2P, yo, k1, k2tog**; rep from ** to ** once; rep from * to * 3 times; rep from ** to ** twice; rep from * to * once, [k2, yo, ssk, yo, SK2P, yo] twice, k2, yo, ssk—150 sts.

Next row (WS) K2, yo, k2tog, *[p3, k2, yo, k2tog] twice, p2*; rep from * to * once, **p3, k2, yo, k2tog, p2**; rep from ** to ** once; rep from * to * 3 times; rep from ** to ** twice; rep from * to * once, [p3, k2, yo, k2tog] twice.

Dec row 6 *[K2, yo, ssk, k3] twice, k2tog*; rep from * to * once, **k2, yo, ssk, k3, k2tog**; rep from ** to ** once; rep from * to * 3 times; rep from ** to ** twice; rep from * to * once, [k2, yo, ssk, k3] twice, k2, yo, ssk—140 sts.

Next row (WS) K2, yo, k2tog, *[p3, k2, yo, k2tog] twice, p1*; rep from * to * once, **p3, k2, yo, k2tog, p1**; rep from ** to ** once; rep from * to * 3 times; rep from ** to ** twice; rep from * to * once, [p3, k2, yo, k2tog] twice.

Dec row 7 [K2, yo, ssk, yo, SK2P, yo] twice, k2tog, k1, yo, ssk, yo, SK2P, yo, k2, yo, ssk, yo, SK2P, yo, k2tog, *k1, yo, ssk, yo, SK2P, yo, k2tog*; rep from * to * once, **k1, yo, ssk, yo, SK2P, yo, k2, yo, ssk, yo, SK2P, yo, k2tog**; rep from ** to ** twice, rep from * to * twice; rep from ** to ** once, k1, yo, ssk, yo, SK2P, yo, k2, yo, ssk, yo, SK2P, yo, k2, yo, ssk—130 sts.

Work rows 2–4 of beehive & faggoting lace pat. Rep rows 1–4 of pat 8 times more.

Next (dec) row *K8, k2tog; rep from * across—117 sts.

Change to garter st (k every row) and bind off 2 sts at the beg of the next 2 rows—113 sts. Knit 3 rows.

COLLAR

Next (inc) row K3, M1, knit across. Rep last row 25 times more—139 sts. Bind off.

FINISHING

CROCHET EDGING

With RS facing and crochet hook, attach yarn to beg of cast-on edge.

Row 1 Ch1, sc in each st across—200 sts.

Row 2 Ch1, sl st in next 2 sts, *ch 3, sl st in last sl st, sl st in next 6 sc; rep from * to last sc, sl st in last sc. Fasten off. Lightly block to measurements.

BUTTONHOLE

With RS facing and crochet hook, attach yarn to right-hand side of capelet, just below collar. Ch 6, sl st in st above and fasten off. Sew button to left-hand side of capelet opposite buttonhole. ●

•Nordic Star

You'll be ready to hit the slopes in any one of CHERYL MURRAY's Scandinavian-inspired neck warmers. All three feature the same two-color Fair Isle motif and are knit in wool, baby alpaca, and angora *Fresco*.

1 The Nordic star pattern anchors either end of this teal and white STRIPED SCARF, which evokes a snowy day in the woods.

2 This melon and cherry ASYMMETRICAL SCARF buttons neatly to stay in place and keep your hands free during winter play.

3 This lovely BUTTONED GAITER is a simple rectangle that buttons neatly around the neck. Contrasting shades of blue and green highlight the Nordic star pattern and flatter the face.

126

37 sts

1 Striped Scarf

KNITTED MEASUREMENTS
Width 9"/23cm
Length 57"/144.5cm

MATERIALS
- 2 1¾oz/50g hanks (each approx 164yd/150m) of Classic Elite Yarns *Fresco* (wool/baby alpaca/angora) each in #5346 mallard blue (A) and #5301 parchment (B) **2**
- One pair size 5 (3.75mm) needles OR SIZE TO OBTAIN GAUGE
- Stitch markers

GAUGE
24 sts and 34 rows = 4"/10cm over St st using size 5 (3.75) needles.
TAKE TIME TO CHECK GAUGE.

NOTE
Nordic Star Chart is worked in St st.

STRIPE PATTERN
In St st, work *2 rows B, 2 rows A; repeat from * for stripe pat. Do not cut

yarn, but carry up along side edge.

SCARF
With A, cast on 51 sts.
Row 1 (RS) K7, place marker (pm), k37, pm, k7.
Row 2 P2, k5, slip marker (sm), k37, sm, k5, p2. Repeat rows 1 and 2 until piece measures 1"/2.5cm from beg, ending with a WS row. Keeping 7 edge sts each side in pat as est, work center 37 sts in St st for 2 rows.
Beg chart (RS) K7, sm, join B and work row 1 of Nordic Star Chart over 37 sts, sm, k7 with A. Keeping 7 edge sts as est and in A, cont in chart pat through row 35.
Next row (WS) Keeping 7 edge sts as est, work center 37 sts in St st for 3 rows with A.
Next row (RS) Keeping 7 edge sts as est

and in stripe pattern, work in stripe pat until piece measures 48"/122cm from beg, ending with stripe A.
Next row (RS) K7, sm, join B and work row 1 of Nordic Star Chart over 37 sts, sm, k7 with A.
Keeping 7 edge sts as est and in A, cont in chart pat through row 35. Keeping 7 edge sts as est, work center 37 sts in St st for 3 rows with A.
Next row (RS) Keeping 7 edge sts as est and in stripe pat, work stripe pat until piece measures 56"/142cm from beg, ending with stripe B. Cut B.
With A and keeping 7 edge sts as est, work in garter st for 1"/2.5cm. Bind off loosely.

FINISHING
Weave in ends. Block lightly. ●

Color Key ☐ A ☐ B

2 Asymmetrical Scarf

KNITTED MEASUREMENTS
Width 8"/20.5cm
Length 38"/96.5cm

MATERIALS
- 2 1¾oz/50g hanks (each approx 164yd/150m) of Classic Elite Yarns *Fresco* (wool/baby alpaca/angora) in #5388 coral (A) (2)
- 1 hank in #5317 sangria (B)
- One pair size 5 (3.75mm) needles OR SIZE TO OBTAIN GAUGE
- One size 5 (3.75mm) circular needle, 49"/122cm long
- One size F/5 (3.75mm) crochet hook
- Three ¹³⁄₁₆"/20mm buttons (Belle Buttons by Dritz #BB348)
- Waste yarn
- Stitch markers

GAUGE
24 sts and 34 rows = 4"/10cm over St st using size 5 (3.75mm) needles. TAKE TIME TO CHECK GAUGE.

NOTE
Nordic Star Chart is worked in St st.

K1, P1 RIB
(worked in the round)
All rnds *K1, p1; rep from *.

STRIPE PATTERN
In St st, work *2 rows B, 2 rows A; repeat from * for stripe pat. Do not cut yarn, but carry up along side edge.

NORDIC STAR CHART

35

30

20

10

1

37 sts

Color Key ▧ A ☐ B

CROCHET CAST-ON
See pg.132
Place a loop on crochet hook. Hold crochet hook in right hand and knitting needle in left hand. Hold working yarn under needle with crochet hook above needle. *With crochet hook, pick up a loop around knitting needle and pull through hook. Place working yarn back under needle; repeat from * until desired number of sts have been cast on.
NOTE For more details about Crochet Cast-on, see "Tutorials/Stitches" section on our website (www.classiceliteyarns).

SCARF

With waste yarn, cast on 37 sts, using the crochet cast-on. With A, work 8 rows in St st.

Beg chart (RS) Attach B and work rows 1–35 of Nordic Star Chart. Cut B and, with A, work 9 rows in St st.

Next row (RS) Begin stripe pat and work until piece measures 29"/73.5cm from beg, ending with stripe B. With A, work 8 rows in St st.

Beg chart (RS) Attach B and work rows 1–35 of Nordic Star Chart. Cut B and, with A, work 9 rows in St st.

Next row (RS) Attach B and work 14 rows in stripe pat.

BORDER

Change to circular needle and A. K across row, place marker (pm), turn slightly, pick up 225 sts along long side of piece, pm, turn slightly, remove waste yarn and knit 37 sts along cast-on edge, pm, turn slightly, pick up 225 sts along remaining long side of piece, pm for beg of rnd—524 sts. Join for working in the round.

Next (inc) rnd K1, M1, *work in k1, p1 rib to next marker, M1, slip marker (sm), k1, M1; rep from * 2 times, work k1, p1 rib to last marker, end M1, sm. Cont in k1, p1 rib, repeating inc rnd every other rnd twice more.

Buttonholes Work 9 sts in rib pat, k2tog, yo; rep from * 2 times more. Cont in rib pat until border measures 1"/2.5cm. Change to B and knit 1 rnd. Bind off loosely.

FINISHING

Weave in ends. Block lightly. With RS facing, sew first button 8"/20.5cm up from bottom edge to right-hand ribbed border, then sew remaining 2 buttons at 1½"/4cm intervals above. ●

③ Buttoned Gaiter

KNITTED MEASUREMENTS
Width 7"/18cm
Length 26"/66cm

MATERIALS
- 1 1¾oz/50g hank (each approx 164yd/150m) of Classic Elite Yarns *Fresco* (wool/baby alpaca/angora) each in #5321 celadon (A) and #5393 cornflower (B) ②
- One pair size 5 (3.75mm) needles, OR SIZE TO OBTAIN GAUGE
- One size 5 (3.75mm) circular needle, 32"/80cm long
- One size F/5 (3.75mm) crochet hook
- Seven ⅝"/15mm buttons (LaMode Buttons #24656)
- Waste yarn
- Stitch markers

GAUGE
24 sts and 34 rows = 4"/10cm over St st, using size 5 (3.75mm) needles.
TAKE TIME TO CHECK GAUGE.

NOTE
Nordic Star Chart is worked in St st.

GARTER STITCH
(worked in the round)
Rnd 1 Knit.
Rnd 2 Purl.
Rep rows 1 and 2 for garter st.

STRIPE PATTERN
In St st, work *2 rows B, 2 rows A; repeat from * for stripe pat. Do not cut yarn, but carry up along side edge.

CROCHET CAST-ON
Place a loop on crochet hook. Hold crochet hook in right hand and knitting needle in left hand. Hold working yarn under needle with crochet hook above needle. *With crochet hook, pick up a loop around knitting needle and pull through hook. Place working yarn back under needle; repeat from * until desired number of sts have been cast on.
NOTE For more details about Crochet Cast-on, see the "Tutorials/Stitches" section on our website (www.classiceliteyarns).

GAITER
With waste yarn, cast on 37 sts using the crochet cast-on.
With A, work 6 rows in St st.
Beg chart (RS) Attach B and work rows 1–35 of Nordic Star Chart (see page 130). Cut B and, with A, work 5 rows in St st.
Begin stripe pat and work until piece measures 24"/61cm from beg, ending with stripe A.

BORDER
Change to circular needle and B, knit across row, place marker (pm). Turn work slightly and pick up 143 sts along long side of piece, pm, turn slightly, remove waste yarn, and knit 37 sts along cast-on edge, pm, turn slightly, pick up 143 sts along remaining long side of piece, pm for beg of rnd—360 sts. Join for working in the round and purl 1 rnd.
Next (inc) rnd: K1, M1, *knit to next marker, M1, slip marker (sm), k1, M1; rep from * 2 times, knit to last marker, end M1, sm. Cont in garter st, repeating inc rnd every other rnd 2 times more. Purl 1 rnd.

ATTACHED I-CORD BIND-OFF
Cast on 2 sts at beg of next rnd.
*K1, ssk, slip 2 sts on right needle back to left needle. Repeat from * along first short edge and 1 long edge, working 1 unattached I-cord at each corner. (To work unattached I-cord, *k2, sl 2 sts back to left needle; rep from * for specified number of sts.)

BUTTONHOLES
Cont I-cord bind off for 2 sts along beg of cast-on edge. *Work 3 unattached I-cord sts, work 6 attached I-cord sts. Repeat from * 6 times more.
Cont attached I-cord bind-off until all sts are bound off. Graft beg and end of I-cord together.

FINISHING
Weave in ends. Block lightly. With RS facing, sew first button to top left-hand corner, then remaining 6 buttons at 1"/25cm intervals down left edge. ●

•Bars & Stripes

JACQUELINE VAN DILLEN's trio of rainbow-bright striped accessories will energize any wardrobe. Worked in garter stitch, they're as easy and fun to knit as they are to wear.

1 With its bold, bright colors, this chunky STRIPED MUFFLER is sure to keep you warm and cheery when the weather is dreary.

2 This BUTTONED WRAP is knit in two pieces and closed in front and back with toggles, allowing for myriad styling options.

3 Double your fun with this easy-to-knit STRIPED INFINITY SCARF by wearing it long or wrapped twice around your neck for extra warmth.

 **Striped Muffler**

KNITTED MEASUREMENTS
Width 7"/18cm
Length 86½"/219.5cm

MATERIALS
- 1 3½oz/100g hank (each approx 87yd/80m) of Classic Elite Yarns *Toboggan* (merino/superfine alpaca) each in #6788 salmon (A), #6731 periwinkle (B), #6732 fuchsia (C), #6746 teal (D), #6750 honey (E), #6794 emerald (F), and #6748 cobalt (G) ⑤
- One pair size 7 (4.5mm) needles OR SIZE TO OBTAIN GAUGE
- Tapestry needle

GAUGE
12 sts and 22 rows = 4"/10cm in garter st using size 7 (4.5mm) needles.
TAKE TIME TO CHECK GAUGE.

STRIPE SEQUENCE
*12 rows A, 4 rows B, 12 rows C, 6 rows D, 16 rows E, 8 rows F, 4 rows G, 12 rows A, 8 rows D, 12 rows G, 12 rows B, 6 rows E, 16 rows C, 12 rows F, 4 rows E, 4 rows G, 16 rows D, 8 rows A, 6 rows E, 12 rows G, 4 rows C, 16 rows B, 16 rows F; rep from * once more.

MUFFLER
Cast on 21 sts with A.
Beg garter stitch (knit every row) in stripe sequence as follows:
Rows 1 (RS) to 12 Knit. Fasten off A and attach B.
Cont in stripe sequence, fastening off after completion of each color and attaching new color. When stripe sequence is completed, bind off all sts with F. Fasten off.

FINISHING
Weave in ends. ●

GAUGE

12½ sts and 23½ rows = 4"/10cm in garter st using size 10 (6mm) needles. TAKE TIME TO CHECK GAUGE.

STRIPE SEQUENCE I

12 rows A, 4 rows B, 12 rows C, 6 rows D, 16 rows E, 8 rows F, 4 rows G, 12 rows A, 8 rows B

STRIPE SEQUENCE II

12 rows G, 12 rows B, 6 rows E, 16 rows C, 12 rows F, 4 rows E, 4 rows G, 16 rows A

PANEL 1

BUTTON BAND

Cast on 65 sts with D. Beg k1, p1 rib:
Row 1 (RS) K1, *p1, k1; rep from* to end.
Row 2 P1, *k1, p1; rep from * to end.
Rows 3–8 Rep rows 1 and 2.
Fasten off D and attach A.

BODY

Beg garter st (knit every row) in stripe sequence I as foll:
Rows 1 (RS) to 12 Knit. Fasten off A and attach B.
Cont in stripe sequence I, fastening off after completion of each color and attaching new color. When stripe sequence I is completed, fasten off B and attach D.

BUTTONHOLE BAND:
Rows 1 and 3 (RS) K1, *p1, k1; rep from * to end.
Row 2 P1, *k1, p1; rep from * to end.
Row 4 (buttonhole) [K1, p1] twice, *K2tog, yo, [k1, p1] 6 times; rep from * 3 times more, k2tog, yo, k1, p1, k1—5 buttonholes made.
Rows 5–7 Work even in rib pat.
Bind off all sts in rib pat. Fasten off.

PANEL 2

Work button band as for panel 1.
Work body as for panel 1 in stripe sequence II.
Work buttonhole band as for panel 1.

FINISHING

With RS of panels 1 and 2 facing, place buttonhole band next to button band. Sew buttons onto button band, positioning same as buttonholes. Rep for opposite button band.
Weave in ends.
Button bands tog to form collar. •

② Buttoned Wrap

KNITTED MEASUREMENTS

Length 21"/53.5cm
Circumference 31"/78.5cm (buttoned)

MATERIALS

- 1 3½oz/100g hank (each approx 109 yd/100m) of Classic Elite Yarns *Verde Collection Sprout* (organic cotton) each in #4392 horizon (A), #4381 mint (B), #4304 chicory (C), #4375 summer rain (D), #4346 glacier (E), #4320 spring breeze (F), and #4331 wisteria (G) ⑤
- One pair size 10 (6mm) needles OR SIZE TO OBTAIN GAUGE
- 10 toggle 2-hole buttons, each 1"/25mm wide, in color A
- Tapestry needle

GAUGE

16¾ sts and 32½ rows = 4"/10cm over garter st using size 7 (4.5mm) needles.

STRIPE SEQUENCE

*12 rows A, 4 rows B, 12 rows C, 6 rows D, 16 rows E, 8 rows F, 4 rows G, 12 rows A, 8 rows D, 12 rows G, 12 rows B, 6 rows E, 16 rows C, 12 rows F, 4 rows E, 4 rows G, 16 rows D**, 8 rows A, 6 rows E, 12 rows G, 4 rows C, 16 rows B, 16 rows F; rep from * once more, then rep bet * and ** once.

COWL

Cast on 40 sts with (A).
Beg garter st (knit every row) in stripe sequence as follows:
Rows 1 (RS) to 12 Knit. Fasten off A and attach B.
Cont in stripe sequence, fastening off after completion of each color and attaching new color. When stripe sequence is completed, bind off all sts with D. Fasten off.

FINISHING

Sew cast-on and bound-off edges tog on WS. Weave in ends. ●

③ Striped Infinity Scarf

KNITTED MEASUREMENTS

Width 9½"/24cm
Length 76"/193cm

MATERIALS

● 1 1¾oz/50g hank (each 110yd/100m) Classic Elite Yarns *Verde Collection Seedling* (organic cotton) each in #4588 persimmon (A), #4558 salvia red (B), #4512 deep saffron (C), #4519 persian rose (D), #4550 evening primrose (E), #4531 wisteria (F), and #4532 vivid fuchsia (G) **(4)**
● One pair size 7 (4.5mm) needles OR SIZE TO OBTAIN GAUGE
● Tapestry needle

•Silk & Cotton

HELEN BINGHAM's set of multiseasonal cover-ups are knit in *Classic Silk*, a blend of cool and soft silk, cotton, and nylon that feels great any time of year.

1 This EYELET COWL features an allover lace pattern and comes to a gentle point in the front for a flattering shape.

2 A simple garter-stitch rectangle is enlivened by leaf stitch and eyelet patterns at either end of this LEAF MOTIF SCARF.

3 This moss-green LEAF PONCHO is knit as a rectangle, then folded and seamed to create a sleeve. The leaf stitch pattern creates a panel flanked by staggered eyelets.

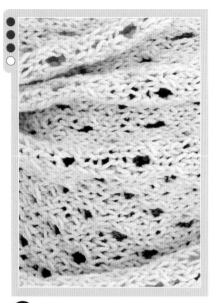

1 Eyelet Cowl

KNITTED MEASUREMENTS
Width approx 11"/28cm,
before seaming
Length approx 35"/89cm,
before seaming
Center front approx 24"/61cm

MATERIALS
- 3 1¾oz/50g balls (each approx 135yd/123m) of Classic Elite Yarns *Classic Silk* (cotton/silk/nylon) in #6916 natural (4)
- One pair size 8 (5mm) needles OR SIZE TO OBTAIN GAUGE
- Size H/8 (5mm) crochet hook (for chain-st provisional cast on)
- Waste yarn

GAUGE
16 sts and 20 rows to 4"/10cm over St st using size 8 (5mm) needles. TAKE TIME TO CHECK GAUGE.

PROVISIONAL CAST-ON
With crochet hook and waste yarn, chain 44 sts. With project yarn, insert size 8 (5mm) needle into first bump from front to back and pick up a st. Continue in this manner until there are 41 sts on needle.
NOTE For more details about Provisional Cast-on, see the "Tutorials/Stitches" section on our website (www.classiceliteyarns).

COWL
Cast on 41 sts using provisional method (see above).
Row 1 (RS) Knit.
Row 2 K3, p35, k3.
Row 3 K3, *k2tog, yo, k2; rep from * to last 6 sts, k2tog, yo, k4.
Rows 4 and 6 Rep row 2.
Row 5 Rep row 1.
Row 7 K3, *k2, k2tog, yo; rep from * to last 6 sts, k6.
Row 8 Rep row 2. Rep rows 1–8 once more.

INCREASE SECTION
Row 1 Knit to last 3 sts, yo, k3—1 st inc.
Row 2 K3, purl to last 3 sts, k3.
Row 3 K3, *k2tog, yo, k2; rep from * to last 7 sts, k2tog, yo, k2, yo, k3—1 st inc.
Rows 4 and 6 Rep row 2.
Row 5 Rep row 1.
Row 7 K3, *k2, k2tog, yo; rep from * to last 5 sts, k2, yo, k3—1 st inc.
Row 8 Rep row 2. Rep rows 1–8 until there are 85 sts, ending with row 8.

DECREASE SECTION
Row 1 Knit to last 6 sts, SK2P, yo, k3—1 st dec.
Row 2 K3, purl to last 3 sts, k3.
Row 3 K3, *k2tog, yo, k2; rep from * to last 9 sts, k2tog, yo, k1, SK2P, yo, k3—1 st dec.
Rows 4 and 6 Rep row 2.
Row 5 Rep row 1.
Row 7 K3, *k2, k2tog, yo; rep from * to last 7 sts, k1, SK2P, yo, k3—1 st dec.
Row 8 Rep row 2. Rep rows 1–8 until there are 41 sts, ending with row 8.

FINAL SECTION
Row 1 (RS) Knit.
Row 2 K3, p35, k3.
Row 3 K3, *k2tog, yo, k2; rep from * to last 6 sts, k2tog, yo, k4.
Rows 4 and 6 Rep row 2.
Row 5 Rep row 1.
Row 7 K3, *k2, k2tog, yo; rep from * to last 6 sts, k6.
Row 8 Rep row 2. Rep rows 1–8 once more. Do not bind off.

FINISHING
Remove waste yarn and place live sts on needle. Graft to last row using kitchener st. Weave in ends and block lightly. ●

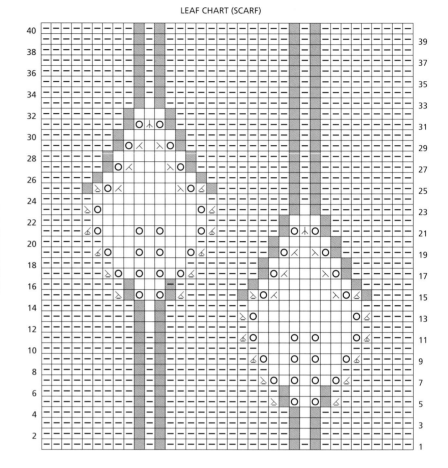

2 Leaf Motif Scarf

KNITTED MEASUREMENTS
Width approx 8"/20.5cm
Length approx 68"/172.5cm

MATERIALS
- 3 1¾oz/50g balls (each approx 135yd/123m) of Classic Elite Yarns *Classic Silk* (cotton/silk/nylon) in #6910 soft violet (**4**)
- One pair size 8 (5mm) needles OR SIZE TO OBTAIN GAUGE
- Waste yarn
- Stitch marker

GAUGE
19 sts and 23 rows to 4"/10cm over St st using size 8 (5mm) needles. TAKE TIME TO CHECK GAUGE.

SCARF HALF (make 2)
Cast on 37 sts. Work in garter st (knit every row) for 5 rows.

Row 1 (RS) Knit.
Row 2 K3, purl to last 3 sts, k3.
Row 3 K3, *k2, k2tog, yo; rep from * to last 6 sts, k6.
Rows 4 and 6 Rep row 2.
Row 5 Knit.
Row 7 K3, *k2tog, yo, k2; rep from * to last 6 sts, k2tog, yo, k4.
Row 8 Rep row 2. Rep rows 1–8 a total of 3 times. Rep rows 1–7 once more.
Next (inc) row (WS) K3, p15, M1, p16, k3—38 sts.
Next row K3, work row 1 of chart, k3.
Next row K3, work row 2 of chart, k3. Continue as set, working rows 1–40 of chart a total of 3 times. Work rows 1–37 of chart once more. Place sts on waste yarn.

FINISHING
Place held sts on needles and join halves using kitchener st. Weave in ends. Block. ●

Stitch Key

☐ K on RS, p on WS	◢ P3tog
☐ P on RS, k on WS	◿ K2tog
Ⓞ Yo	◺ Ssk
◿ P2tog	⋏ SK2P
◺ Ssp	▦ No stitch

GAUGE

16 sts and 20 rows to 4"/10cm over St st using size 8 (5mm) needles
TAKE TIME TO CHECK GAUGE.

STITCH GLOSSARY

Ssp (slip, slip, purl)
Slip 2 sts, 1 at a time, knitwise to RH needle; return sts to LH needle in turned position and purl them together through the back loops (1 st decreased).

STAGGERED EYELET PAT

Rows 1 and 5 (RS) Knit.
Row 2 and all WS rows Purl.
Row 3 K2, *k2tog, yo, k2; rep from * to last st, k1.
Row 7 K2tog, yo, *k2, k2tog, yo; rep from * to last st, k1.
Row 8 Purl.
Rep rows 1–8 for pat.

PONCHO

Cast on 89 sts.
Set-up row (WS) K2, p15, pm, k39, pm, p31, k2.
Next row (RS) K2, work row 1 of staggered eyelet pat to marker, slip marker, work row 1 of leaf chart to next marker, slip marker, work to last 2 sts in staggered eyelet pat, k2.
Next row K2, work row 2 of staggered eyelet pat to marker, slip marker, work row 2 of leaf chart to next marker, slip marker, work to last 2 sts in staggered eyelet pat, k2. Continue as set, working rows 1–48 of leaf chart a total of 7 (8) times. Bind off in pat.

FINISHING

Fold in half lengthwise, with fold on left and cast-on and bound-off edges tog on the right, and 15-st wide eyelet portion at upper edge. Beg at top right corner, sew along top edge for 20½ (24)"/52 (61)cm, leaving an opening for neck. For the sleeve, beg at the lower right corner, sew along lower edge for 5 (7)"/12.5 (18)cm. Weave in ends. Block lightly. ●

❸ Leaf Poncho

SIZES

S/M (L/XL) to fit
30–38 (40–48)"/76–96.5
(101.5–122)cm bust; shown in size S/M.

KNITTED MEASUREMENTS

Width approx 22¼"/56.5cm, before seaming
Length approx 61½ (70)"/156 (177.5)cm, before seaming

MATERIALS

● 7 (8) 1¾oz/50g balls (each approx 135yd/123m) of Classic Elite Yarns *Classic Silk* (cotton/silk/nylon) in #6972 moss (⓸)
● One pair size 8 (5mm) needles OR SIZE TO OBTAIN GAUGE
● Stitch marker

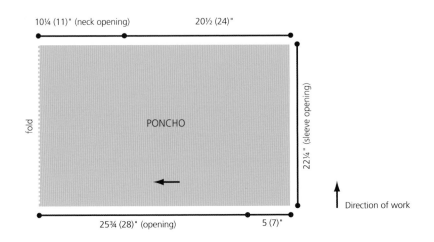

10¼ (11)" (neck opening)   20½ (24)"

fold

PONCHO

22¼" (sleeve opening)

Direction of work

25¾ (28)" (opening)   5 (7)"

3 Leaf Poncho

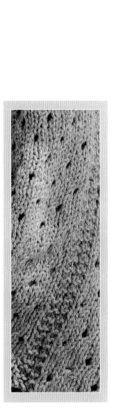

LEAF CHART (PONCHO)

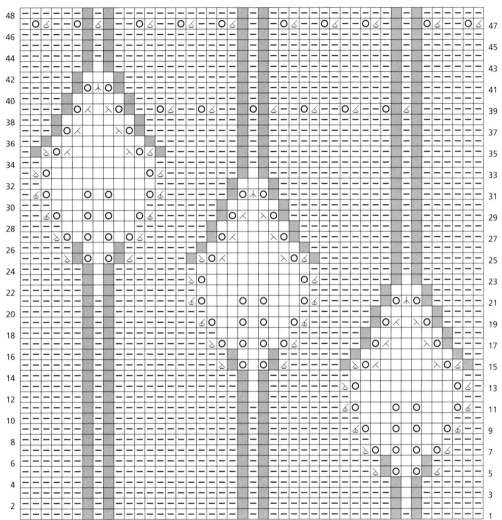

39 sts

STAGGERED EYELET CHART

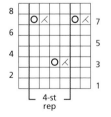

4-st rep

Stitch Key

☐	K on RS, p on WS	
—	P on RS, k on WS	
O	Yo	
◿	P2tog	
◸	Ssp	

◿	P3tog
◿	K2tog
◼	Ssk
⼐	SK2P
▨	No stitch

•Cream & Sugar

ANNIKEN ALLIS takes three yarns in delicate shades of white and whips them into three gorgeous confections. The same beautiful lace stitch is showcased in each.

1 This feminine LACE COWL in kid mohair, bamboo, and nylon viscose, *Pirouette* is a lovely accessory to take you from autumn through spring. The allover lacework makes it light enough to wear indoors.

2 This sweet LACE SHAWLETTE is knit in luscious cream-colored baby alpaca and bamboo *Vail*. The complexity of the lace pattern and insertion is tempered with triangular patches of garter stitch.

3 Meltingly soft *Vail* in a shade reminiscent of burnt sugar creates a splendid LACE WRAP for spring.

1/2

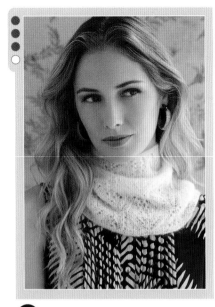

KNITTED MEASUREMENTS

Circumference 28"/71cm
Length 10"/25.5cm

MATERIALS

- 2 0.88oz/25g balls (each approx 246yd/225m) of Classic Elite Yarns *Pirouette* (kid mohair/bamboo viscose-nylon) in #4016 natural ⓵
- One size 4 (3.5mm) circular needle, 24"/60cm long, OR SIZE TO OBTAIN GAUGE
- Stitch marker

GAUGE

One 22-st pattern rep of Chart 1 measures 3"/7.5cm long and 4"/10cm wide using size 4 (3.5mm) needles, after blocking.
TAKE TIME TO CHECK GAUGE.

COWL

Cast on 154 sts. Place marker for beg of rnd and join being careful not to twist sts. Work 4 rnds in garter st (k1 rnd, p1 rnd).

BEG CHART

Rnd 1 Work 22-st rep of chart 1 seven times around.
Cont to work chart in this manner until 28 rows have been worked 3 times. Work 4 rnds in garter st. Bind off loosely.

FINISHING

Weave in ends. Pin wet cowl to measurements and let dry. ●

1 Lace Cowl

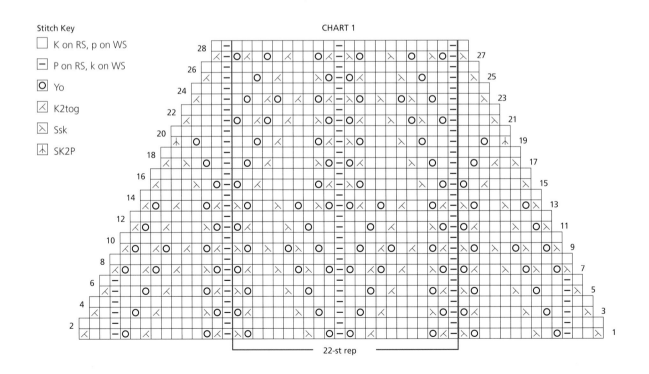

CHART 1

Stitch Key

- ☐ K on RS, p on WS
- ⊟ P on RS, k on WS
- ⊙ Yo
- ⊠ K2tog
- ⊠ Ssk
- ⊠ SK2P

22-st rep

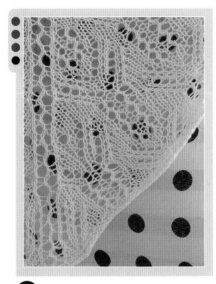

2 Lace Shawlette

KNITTED MEASUREMENTS
Width 56"/142cm
Length 28"/71cm

MATERIALS
● 2 1¾oz/50g hanks (each approx 236yd/216m) of Classic Elite Yarns *MountainTop Vail* (baby alpaca/bamboo viscose) in #6416 parchment
● One size 6 (4mm) circular needle, 24"/60cm long, OR SIZE TO OBTAIN GAUGE

GAUGES
17 sts and 32 rows over garter st using size 6 (4mm) needle.
One 22-st/28-row pattern rep of Chart 1 measures 5½"/14cm wide and 3½"/9cm long after blocking.

SPINE PATTERN
(over a multiple of 2 sts)
Row 1 Yo, ssk.
Row 2 Purl.
Row 3 K2tog, yo.
Row 4 Purl. Rep rows 1–4 for spine pat.

SHAWLETTE
Cast on 284 sts. Knit 1 row.
Next row (WS) Sl 1, k to end.
Rep last row 2 times more.

BEG CHART 1
Row 1 (RS) Sl 1, k1, *work to rep line, work 22-st rep 5 times across, work to end of chart*, work row 1 of spine pat, rep from * to * once more, k2.
Row 2 Sl 1, k1, *work to rep line, work 22-st rep 5 times across, work to end of chart*, work row 2 of spine pat, rep from * to * once more, k2.
Cont to work chart in this manner until row 28 is complete. Cont in pats, working decs as established and rep rows 1–28 once more, then rows 1–14 once over 22-st rep—144 sts.

BEG GARTER ST PAT
Next row (RS) Sl 1, k1, ssk, k to 2 sts before spine pat, k2tog, work spine pat, ssk, k to last 4 sts, k2tog, k2.
Next row Sl 1, k to spine pat, work spine pat, k to end. Rep last 2 rows 32 times more, end with a WS row—12 sts.

SHAPE NECK
Next row (RS) Sl 1, SK2P, work spine pat, SK2P, k2—8 sts.
Next row Sl 1, k to end.
Next row SK2P, k2, SK2P—4 sts.
Next row Sl 1, k to end.
Next row Sl 2, k2tog, pass slipped sts over the resulting st. Fasten off.

FINISHING
Weave in ends. Pin wet shawl to measurements and let dry to block. ●

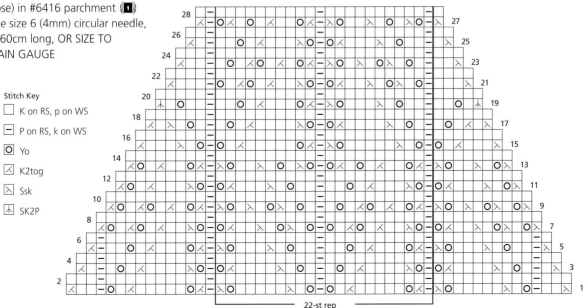

CHART 1

Stitch Key
□ K on RS, p on WS
— P on RS, k on WS
O Yo
╱ K2tog
╲ Ssk
⅄ SK2P

22-st rep

155

GAUGE

One 22-st 28=row pattern rep of Chart 1 measures 5½"/14cm wide and 3½"/9cm long using size 6 (4mm) needles, after blocking.
TAKE TIME TO CHECK GAUGE.

WRAP

Cast on 79 sts.
Next row Sl 1, k to end.
Rep last row 3 times more.

BEG CHARTS

Row 1 (RS) Sl 1, k1, work Chart 2 over next 15 sts, work 22-st rep of Chart 1 twice, p1, work Chart 2 over next 15 sts, k2.
Row 2 Sl 1, k1, work Chart 2 over next 15 sts, k1, work 22-st rep of Chart 1 twice, work Chart 2 over next 15 sts, k2.
Cont to work charts in this manner until the 28 rows of Chart 1 have been worked 12 times and the 14 rows of

Chart 2 have been worked 24 times.
Knit 4 rows.
Bind off as foll:
K2, *sl both sts back to LH needle, k2tog tbl, k1; rep from * until all sts are bound off. Fasten off.

FINISHING

Weave in ends. Pin wet shawl to measurements and let dry to block. ●

③ Lace Wrap

KNITTED MEASUREMENTS

Width approx 17"/43cm
Length approx 50 "/126cm

MATERIALS

● 3 1¾oz/50g hanks (each approx 236yd/216m) of Classic Elite Yarns *MountainTop Vail* (baby alpaca/bamboo viscose) in #6436 sand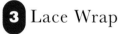
● One pair size 6 (4mm) needles OR SIZE TO OBTAIN GAUGE

Stitch Key

☐ K on RS, p on WS

⊟ P on RS, k on WS

[O] Yo

[◺] K2tog

[◿] Ssk

[⋏] SK2P

CHART 2

CHART 1

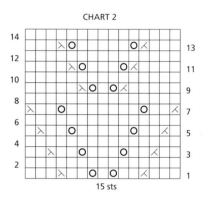

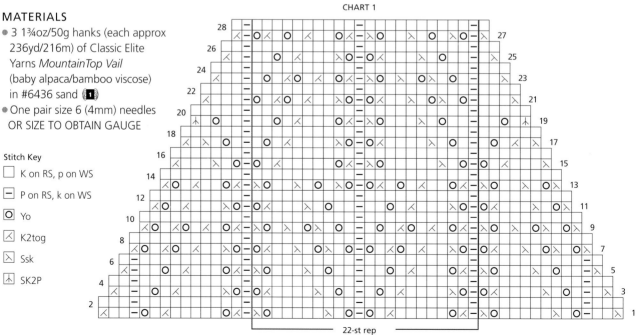

•Helpful Information

Abbreviations

approx	approximately	rep	repeat	St st	stockinette stitch
beg	begin(ning)	RH	right-hand	tbl	through back
CC	contrasting color	RS	right side(s)		loop(s)
ch	chain	rnd(s)	round(s)	tog	together
cm	centimeter(s)	SKP	slip 1, knit 1, pass	WS	wrong side(s)
cn	cable needle		slip st over (one st	wyib	with yarn in back
cont	continu(e)(ing)		has been	wyif	with yarn in front
dec	decreas(e)(ing)		decreased)	yd	yard(s)
dpn	double-pointed	SK2P	slip 1, knit 2 tog,	yo	yarn over needle
	needle(s)		pass	*	repeat directions
foll	follow(s)(ing)		slip st over the		following*
g	gram(s)		knit 2 tog (two sts	[ ]	repeat directions
inc	increas(e)(ing)		have been		inside brackets as
k	knit		decreased)		many times as
k2tog	knit 2 sts tog	S2KP	slip 2 sts tog, knit		indicated
	(one st has been		1, pass 2 slip sts		
	decreased)		over knit 1 (two		
LH	left-hand		sts have been		
lp(s)	loop(s)		decreased)		
m	meter(s)	sl	slip		
mm	millimeter(s)	sl st	slip stitch		
MC	main color	ssk	slip 2 sts kwise,		
M1	make one st; with		one at a time;		
	needle tip, lift		insert tip of		
	strand between		LH needle into		
	last st knit		front of these sts		
	and next st on LH		and knit them		
	needle and knit		tog (one st has		
	into back of it		been decreased)		
M1 p-st	make 1 purl st	sssk	slip 3 sts kwise,		
oz	ounce(s)		one at a time;		
p	purl		insert tip of		
pat(s)	pattern(s)		front of these sts		
pm	place marker		and knit them		
psso	pass slip stitch(es)		tog (two sts have		
	over		been decreased)		
rem	remain(s)(ing)	st(s)	stitch(es)		

Knitting Needles

U.S.	Metric
0	2mm
1	2.25mm
2	2.75mm
3	3.25mm
4	3.5mm
5	3.75mm
6	4mm
7	4.5mm
8	5mm
9	5.5mm
10	6mm
10½	6.5mm
11	8mm
13	9mm
15	10mm
17	12.75mm
19	15mm
35	19mm

Skill Levels

● **1** Beginner
Ideal first project.

● **2** Easy
Basic stitches, minimal shaping, and simple finishing.

● **3** Intermediate
For knitters with some experience. More intricate stitches, shaping, and finishing.

● **4** Experienced
For knitters able to work patterns with complicated shaping and finishing.

Metric Conversions To convert measurements from inches to centimeters, simply multiply by 2.54.

Gauge

Make a test swatch at least 4"/10cm square. If the number of stitches and rows does not correspond to the gauge given, you must change the needle size.

An easy rule to follow is: To get fewer stitches to the inch/cm, use a larger needle; to get more stitches to the inch/cm, use a smaller needle. Continue to try different needle sizes until you get the same number of stitches in the gauge.

Stitches measured over 4"/5cm.

Rows measured over 4"/5cm.

STANDARD YARN WEIGHT SYSTEM

Categories of yarn, gauge ranges, and recommended needle and hook sizes

Yarn Weight Symbol & Category Names	**0** Lace	**1** Super Fine	**2** Fine	**3** Light	**4** Medium	**5** Bulky	**6** Super Bulky
Type of Yarns in Category	Fingering 10 count crochet thread	Sock, Fingering, Baby	Sport, Baby	DK, Light Worsted	Worsted, Afghan, Aran	Chunky, Craft, Rug	Bulky, Roving
Knit Gauge Range* in Stockinette Stitch to 4 inches	33–40** sts	27–32 sts	23–26 sts	21–24 sts	16–20 sts	12–15 sts	6–11 sts
Recommended Needle in Metric Size Range	1.5–2.25 mm	2.25–3.25 mm	3.25–3.75 mm	3.75–4.5 mm	4.5–5.5 mm	5.5–8 mm	8 mm and larger
Recommended Needle U.S. Size Range	000 to 1	1 to 3	3 to 5	5 to 7	7 to 9	9 to 11	11 and larger
Crochet Gauge* Ranges in Single Crochet to 4 inch	32–42 double crochets**	21–32 sts	16–20 sts	12–17 sts	11–14 sts	8–11 sts	5–9 sts
Recommended Hook in Metric Size Range	Steel*** 1.6–1.4mm Regular hook 2.25 mm	2.25–3.5 mm	3.5–4.5 mm	4.5–5.5 mm	5.5–6.5 mm	6.5–9 mm	9 mm and larger
Recommended Hook U.S. Size Range	Steel*** 6, 7, 8 Regular hook B–1	B/1 to E/4	E/4 to 7	7 to I/9	I/9 to K/10½	K/10½ to M/13	M/13 and larger

* Guidelines only: The above reflect the most commonly used gauges and needle or hook sizes for specific yarn categories.

** Lace-weight yarns are usually knitted or crocheted on larger needles and hooks to create lacy, openwork patterns. Accordingly, a gauge range is difficult to determine. Always follow the gauge stated in your pattern.

*** Steel crochet hooks are sized differently from regular hooks—the higher the number, the smaller the hook, which is the reverse of regular hook sizing.

Yarn Resource | All the yarns used in this book are available online at Classic Elite Yarns in the "Where to Buy" section: http://classiceliteyarns.com/wheretobuy.php

•Index